Playtime Poets
Edited by Mark Richardson

First published in Great Britain in 2006 by:
Young Writers
Remus House
Coltsfoot Drive
Peterborough
PE2 9JX
Telephone: 01733 890066
Website: www.youngwriters.co.uk

All Rights Reserved

© Copyright Contributors 2006

SB ISBN 1 84602 555 9

Foreword

Young Writers was established in 1991 and has been passionately devoted to the promotion of reading and writing in children and young adults ever since. The quest continues today. Young Writers remains as committed to the nurturing of poetic and literary talent as ever.

This year's Young Writers competition has proven as vibrant and dynamic as ever and we are delighted to present a showcase of the best poetry from across the UK and in some cases overseas. Each poem has been selected from a wealth of *A Pocketful Of Rhyme* entries before ultimately being published in this, our fourteenth primary school poetry series.

Once again, we have been supremely impressed by the overall quality of the entries we have received. The imagination, energy and creativity which has gone into each young writer's entry made choosing the poems a challenging and often difficult but ultimately hugely rewarding task - the general high standard of the work submitted ensured this opportunity to bring their poetry to a larger appreciative audience.

We sincerely hope you are pleased with this final collection and that you will enjoy *A Pocketful Of Rhyme Playtime Poets* for many years to come.

Contents

Nirvana Eden (11)	1
George Ball (8)	2
Katie Rees (11)	3

Alban Wood Primary & Nursery School, Watford

Tegan Kenney (11)	4
Jamie Chapman (11)	4
Katharine Richardson (11)	5
Amy Woods (11)	5
Stephanie Christensen (11)	6
Tom Walker (11)	6
Sadie Norris (11)	6
Kayleigh Down (11)	7
Lewis Edwards (11)	7
John Smith (11)	7
Brooke Holliman (11)	8
Kerry-Lee O'Mahony (11)	8
Hannah Greene (11)	8
Beth Yates (10)	9
Armani Pereira-Grieves (11)	9
Heshawa Abayatilaka (11)	9
Jessica Maxwell (11)	10
Olivia Eze (11)	10
Jessica Dabhade (10)	10
Natasha Brewer (11)	11

All Saints CE First School, Morpeth

Jack Stanners (9)	11
Ashleigh Platt (9)	11
Katie Littlewood (9)	12
James Statton (9)	12
Beth Sproston (9)	13
Alexandra Durance (9)	13
Alison Russo (9)	14
Curtis Jeffery (9)	14
Lauren Wigham (9)	15

Barton CE Primary School, Barton

Savannah Bennett (10)	15
Andrew Healy (11)	16
Amy Wilkins (10)	16
Georgia Smith (10)	16
Cally Saul (9)	17
Toni Hardy (9)	17
Matthew Ellis (11)	17
Sophie Bates (9)	18
Rebecca Woor (10)	18
Joel Saul (13)	19
James Prince (9)	19
Alan Hall (10)	20
Abigail Johnson (10)	20
Sarah Pedder (10)	21
Emma Bithell (9)	21
Ryan Chamberlain-Cox (11)	22
Josh Nathan (11)	22
Sophie Martin (11)	23

Benhurst Primary School, Hornchurch

Sarah Wingett, Rebecca Millward, Emily Grimes (11) & Abbie Schafer (10)	24
Emma Askew, Joshua Birch (10) & Ellen Glazebrook (9)	25
Emma Hankin (10) & Eva Ahern (9)	26
Rosie Wallace, Lucy Austin (10) & Hannah Clements (9)	27
Amy Johns & Molly Tyler (11)	28
Joe Groves & Liam Mercer (10)	29
Alexandra Georgiou (10)	30
Joe Kavanagh & Joe Williams (10)	31
Ebele Nwangwu & Bethany Humphrey (11)	32

Blackdale County Middle School, Norwich

Sophie Childerhouse & Kayleigh Watts (10)	33
Danielle Haycock (10)	34
Marcus Kerton & Ross Schuller (10)	34
Bethany Chapman (10)	35
Sophie Aldous & Jessica Chester (9)	35

Blakesley CE Primary School, Blakesley
Imogen Mintram (10)	36
Beth Mintram (10)	36
Abigail Chambers (10)	36
Charles Getter (10)	37
Ryan Gyles (10)	37

Brilley CE School, Whitney
Ben Wright (10)	37
Laura Wright (8)	38
Ethan Roberts (8)	38
Jamie Jerman (9)	38
Lister Morris (11)	39
Hattie Roberts (10)	39
David Price (11)	39
Ben Woolley (8)	40
Lucinda Jones (11)	40
Amy Griffiths (11)	40

Buxton CP School, Norwich
Amber Glaysher (9)	41
Hayden Ramm	41
Daniel Rivett (10)	41
Jake Webster	42
Megan Taylor (9)	43
Taylor de Lucchi (9)	43
Jamie Barnes (10)	44
Adam Gray (10)	44
Joshua Overton (10)	45
Chloe Gowen (10)	45
Katharine Butchers (10)	46
Tom Booth (9)	46
Emma Waller (9)	47
James Douglas	47
Harry Dread	48

Chesterfield Junior School, Enfield
Paris Demetriou (9)	48

City of London School for Girls, London
   Maddy Richardson (11)   49

Harlesden Primary School, London
   Mustafa C Kherbane (9)   50
   Sokaina Zaari (9)   50
   Mital Pratap (9)   51
   Abdikafi Dahir (9)   51
   Anam Parveen (8)   52
   Jay Pratap (9)   52
   Simon Fatimehin (9)   53
   Alyah Sharifah Lewis (9)   53
   Nur Mohamed (9)   54
   Anthony O'Connor (9)   54
   Nikita Braithwaite & Anisa Abdul-Kadir (9)   55
   Ladana Mohamed Awil   55
   Sananthen Balaskander   56
   Ryan Dolling (9)   56
   Julio Pashollari (9)   56

Keble Prep School, London
   Luke Simmons (8)   57
   Bolaji Anifalaje (8)   57
   Nana Antwi (9)   58
   Rhys Beacham (8)   59
   Mohsin Abedi (9)   60
   Tomi Badmos (9)   60
   Adeniran Thompson (9)   61
   Charlie Pearch (9)   61
   Anthony Constantinou (9)   62
   Sebastian Davis (8)   63
   Thomas Matthews (9)   64
   George Newton (8)   65
   Savvas Petrou (9)   66
   Bhavek Shah (9)   67
   Zachary Woodhouse (9)   68
   Henry Jeffery (9)   69
   Oliver Keane (9)   70

Langham Primary School, Langham
    Connor Baird (8)   70

Maldon Primary School, Maldon
    Pierce Rannigan (9)   71
    Amy Rolfe (9)   71
    Jake Gilroy (8)   72
    Bethany Williams (8)   72
    Joel Manning (9)   73
    Ashley Green (8)   73
    Amie Bridge (8)   74
    Calum Banks (9)   74
    Thomas Parmenter (9)   75
    Rebecca Buchanan (8)   75
    Beth Elsegood (9)   76
    Max Dee (9)   76
    Lucy Maynard (9)   77
    Jodie Butler (9)   77
    James Dickson (9)   78
    Corrin Jelbart (9)   78
    Amy Harrison (9)   79
    Jasmine Linge (8)   79
    Joanna Crellin (9)   80
    Ella-Mae Potter (8)   80
    Talasi Howell-Cole (8)   81
    Amy Curtis (8)   81
    Kiera Howell (8)   82

Orchard Way Primary School, Croydon
    Ryan Whitehead (8)   83
    Angela Petrassei (8)   84
    Abbie Thompson (9)   85
    Rebecca Schneider (9)   85
    Becky Ward (8)   85

Rockingham Primary School, Corby
    Jake Saunders (8)   86
    Elliott Chapman (8)   86
    Chloe Morrison (8)   87
    Evan Williams (8)   87

Jack Moir (8)	88
Bethanie Forbes (7)	88

SS Peter & Paul RC School, London

Jessica Hammond (10)	89
Kristian Medina (10)	90
Kimberley-Anne Laylo (10)	90
Ashleigh Jones (9)	91
Juan David Tenorio (10)	91
Lauren Wirrich (10)	92
Joe Scanlan (10)	93
Stephen Amat (10)	93
Ella Adkins (10)	94
Connor Homer-Deegan (10)	94
Holly Dowling (10)	95
Marley Christian Pompilio (10)	95
Megan McDonald-Marshall (10)	96
Oliver Togias (9)	96
Simone Mari (9)	97
Rosie Brooks (10)	97
Pauline Villar (10)	98
Claudia McCarthy (10)	98
Elliott Fredrick (10)	99
Julia Mari (10)	99
Vanessa Zipagan (10)	100

St Alban's Catholic Primary School, Hornchurch

Korede Falebita (7)	100
Christopher Joseph Caballero (7)	101
Michael Webb (7)	102

St Cuthbert's RC Primary School, Walbottle

Matthew Collins (10)	102
Jessica Hodge (10)	103
Jenny Brown (11)	103
James Hall (10)	104
Georgia Stone (11)	104
Francesca Giuliani (11)	105
Chloe Kendal (11)	105
Chalon Collingwood (11)	106

Katherine McKeen (11)	106
Alexander Dundon (10)	107
Arran Yau (11)	107

St Joseph's RC Primary School, Waltham Cross
Alannah Taylor (9)	108

Stamford Hill Primary School, London
Mahfuzur Rahman (10)	109
Ayanna Tafial-Novella (10)	109
Altiman James Jnr (11)	110
Kenny Tran (11)	110
Ahkeisha Brown (11)	111
Meezan Paul (10)	111
Davika Gravillis (11)	112
Kadiatu Kamara (11)	113

Thomas Fairchild Community School, London
Gold Class (Year 4)	114

Thorpedene Junior School, Shoeburyness
Elle Russell (8)	114
Tyler Crawley (11)	115
Jenna Waterman (8)	115
Laura Joseph (8)	116

The Poems

My Mum

My mum is sometimes happy
Sometimes even chatty

My mum is sometimes sad
And sometimes gets mad

My mum is sometimes funny
And makes me feel sunny

My mum is a light
That's really, really bright

My mum is the water
And I am her daughter

My mum is the rain
And sometimes is in pain

My mum is made of love
She is as pretty as a dove

My mum is the best
She is better than all the rest.

Nirvana Eden (11)

A Timeline Of My Life

Where is that baby that used to crawl when I was one?
All grown up and zooming about.
Where is my sister that popped out of my mum's tummy
when I was two?
Six years old and walking about.
Where is my tooth that popped out of my gum when I was three?
Sleeping warmly in the tooth fairy's hand.
Where is that country I went to when I was four?
Floating about and shaking the sea.
Where is Thailand, the place I went to when I was five?
Building more and better things.
Where did Mum go when she passed away when I was six?
Floating in Heaven, smiling away.
Where is that bird I set free when I was seven?
Flying away to my old mum.
Where did my old house go when I was eight?
Standing still in all the weathers.

George Ball (8)

My Sisters

I once had a sister I knew,
Who sat with me in the church pew,
We were good friends for years,
Although we often shed tears,
But she was the sister I knew.

Years passed by,
Our friendship did fly,
And then a new one was born,
We were now a threesome,
But were often quite tearsome,
But they were the sisters I knew.

I love them both dearly,
Although I often speak to them severely,
But I love them both just the same,
One sucks her thumb,
The others says 'bum',
But they are the sisters I know.

Katie Rees (11)

Oops!

I am Tegan and I'm 11 years old,
Oops, oh no! I stepped in mould.
I like chocolate, but don't eat much,
Oh, there's some crisps, I'd better not touch.
Oops, oh no! I got gum on my shoe,
Oh, what should I do?

Why do all the bad things always happen to me?
But now I'm on a roller coaster, *wheee!*
Oops, oh no! I fell over a brick.
Oh no, now I feel sick.

Oops, oh no! that's all I do.
Does it ever happen to you?
Wait a minute, I'm in luck,
As I am not stuck.
Unlike my dad in a traffic queue!

Oops, oh no is me no more,
I'm sure.

Tegan Kenney (11)
Alban Wood Primary & Nursery School, Watford

White Horse

The waves are still and silent,
No wind, no rain, not even a ripple.
Suddenly the wind picks up,
Shifting the waves onto the beach.
As the waves roll,
Three white horses ride on the waves.
They try to put their hooves on the sand,
But they just crash and dissolve.
The white horses are dead,
Thanks to the golden grains of sand.

Jamie Chapman (11)
Alban Wood Primary & Nursery School, Watford

Sums

She ran through the corridor,
Quickly and swiftly,
Bashing open all the doors,
Sleek and nifty.

She stopped with a start,
She turned and walked the other way,
As she saw the bully coming towards her,
Oh, what a miserable day.

She walked along,
Doing sums in her head,
But when she added them up,
It equalled her loneliness and dread.

Katharine Richardson (11)
Alban Wood Primary & Nursery School, Watford

Bed Without Tea

I was sent to bed without tea!
But it was definitely not me,
Who threw the ball at the vase
(And knocked down several jars).
Anyway I went to bed in a mood,
Because I wasn't getting any food.
So what did I dream when I fell asleep?
Sugar-coated biscuits sprinkled with sweets!
Chocolate-covered toffees, *mmmm* delicious,
Although they're not very nutritious.
I dreamt of food until it was dawning,
When I woke up I realised it was morning.
I rushed downstairs to finally eat,
So I could have ten bowls of shredded wheat!

Amy Woods (11)
Alban Wood Primary & Nursery School, Watford

It's Literacy, Oh No!

My teacher asked me to write a poem,
I just can't,
I don't know where to start.
When I do try I'm lost
And don't know what to write.
I feel myself getting more and more upset,
Then I taste the tears that start to fall
From my eyes and run down my face.

Stephanie Christensen (11)
Alban Wood Primary & Nursery School, Watford

Arsenal

A ssassinate the nearest team
R un the field like a lightning beam
S kilful players like Thierry Henry
E ven players like van Persie
N ever easy to beat
A lways winning because we're the Gunners
L ike to own all the fast runners.

Tom Walker (11)
Alban Wood Primary & Nursery School, Watford

Fantasy

Magical wands whirling,
Unicorn tails whipping,
Troublesome trolls chanting,
Pine tree pixies dancing,
Wicked witches cursing,
Sugar plum fairies singing.
    All in the world of dreams . . .
    Only in the world of dreams.

Sadie Norris (11)
Alban Wood Primary & Nursery School, Watford

Kids

Kids dress cool
Kids are tall
Kids think they know it all
Kids don't obey the rules
Kids like to play the fool

Kids don't eat their greens
Kids can be mean
Kids like to go to the mall
And shop and shop until their bags are full.

Kayleigh Down (11)
Alban Wood Primary & Nursery School, Watford

Who's This Footballer?

Brazilian thunder
Barcelona striker
Red and blue shirt
White and gold boots
Greatest footballer in the world
Brown, curly hair
Smashing goal scorer
Who am I?

Lewis Edwards (11)
Alban Wood Primary & Nursery School, Watford

World Cup!

We're ready for the World Cup
So everybody get up
And cheer on our team
Rooney will run around you like a beam
We can play Brazil
And then we'll chill
For the World Cup we will win.

John Smith (11)
Alban Wood Primary & Nursery School, Watford

Dolphins

D olphins like to do tricks
O ver a big hoop and ditch
L ong way forward to the sea
P eople like to have a fantasy of dolphins under the sea
H orrid hunters hunt for dolphins
I n boats sailing the ocean
N aughty sharks try to catch them
S and sinks with a dolphin.

Brooke Holliman (11)
Alban Wood Primary & Nursery School, Watford

Early In The Morning

As the sun rose into the blue sky
After a long sleep everything tinged gold
The blades of grass stood up and swayed gently
As the wind raced by
The flowers uncurled their petals
To say hello to the sun
And the trees swayed happily.

Kerry-Lee O'Mahony (11)
Alban Wood Primary & Nursery School, Watford

Dream

I had a bad dream
And it was really mean.
I tossed about
With a loud shout.
I woke up with a fright
So I turned on my bright light.

Hannah Greene (11)
Alban Wood Primary & Nursery School, Watford

The Seaside

S aturdays I like to go to the seaside
E ating food by the tide
A re you ready to go?
S and everywhere between my toes
I n the sea it's very cold
D ad got me a lilo which was gold
E verybody at the seaside.

Beth Yates (10)
Alban Wood Primary & Nursery School, Watford

Moon

Powdery moon
Sun will come soon
Then comes sunset
Smell of perfume
We will dance all day
And make our way
And dance back into the moon.

Armani Pereira-Grieves (11)
Alban Wood Primary & Nursery School, Watford

Snake

Slithers and slides
Sneaks and hides
He digs his fangs into mice
And by night they're as cold as ice
Their heartbeats get slower
And everything gets fainter
By morning there is no trace.

Heshawa Abayatilaka (11)
Alban Wood Primary & Nursery School, Watford

Birthday

B irthdays are celebrations
I nstead of doing nothing for a birthday
R hyming on your birthday is fun
T o do with someone like you
H ave fun on a birthday
D o you have fun?
A ll day eat cake
Y our birthday comes once a year.

Jessica Maxwell (11)
Alban Wood Primary & Nursery School, Watford

Magical

Fairies and flies
That twirl in the skies
Pixies and trolls
Butterflies and lost souls
Purple, red and green
Dance around on the magical scene
Through the forest trees
Lurk the sparkling seas
In the world of magic.

Olivia Eze (11)
Alban Wood Primary & Nursery School, Watford

Lion

Shy lions purr around
Let me see you twirl
In diamonds and pears
You roar out loud
With a noisy sound
And like to be proud.

Jessica Dabhade (10)
Alban Wood Primary & Nursery School, Watford

Christmas

C hristmases are so great
H ear Dad singing while putting up the tree
R esting in bed waiting for Christmas
I n the garden playing in the snow
S melling Mum's lovely cookies cooking
T asting a drop of snow in your mouth
M aking snowmen with Mum and Dad
A t the shops waiting for Mum and Dad
S adly, Christmas is over now. I have to wait till next year.

Natasha Brewer (11)
Alban Wood Primary & Nursery School, Watford

Snowboard Morning

The high up mountain
All covered in snow
The snowboarder lies low
Waiting for the moment the cockerel will crow
The cockerel starts to howl as the snowboarder starts to scowl
He gets up for the race at a steady pace.

Jack Stanners (9)
All Saints CE First School, Morpeth

Speed Run

Fast, hard hitting
Fun with speed
Slippy and skiddy
Scary, never slow

Windy, cool and very cold
But wild tunnels
Are not the half of it!

Ashleigh Platt (9)
All Saints CE First School, Morpeth

The Twinkling Ice!

When my feet touch that ice,
The twinkling water makes me shiver.
I spring around, up and down
And then I start to quiver.

I drift silently across the ice,
Avoiding parts that are slippery.
The shiny ice below my feet,
Exciting and twinkling.

No! I can't hold my balance,
The ice is too slippery.
I'm going to fall, quickly,
Please help me somebody.

My sister pushes me over,
She says she is sorry.
I am hurt very much,
But I accept her apology.

Katie Littlewood (9)
All Saints CE First School, Morpeth

Snowboarding - Haikus

The fast, speedy men
Like to soar through the cold air
Up and down the ramps.

They slide perfectly
Across the beautiful snow
And they should get gold.

Sliding, gliding, well
Jumping high into the sky
But who will get gold?

James Statton (9)
All Saints CE First School, Morpeth

Ice Skating

The beautiful woman
Gracefully glided across
The shiny, white ice.

Her jazzy dress glittered
In the bright light
Sequins stuck hard to
Her sleeves.

Her boots had chips
Of hard, cold ice,
Freezing fast and
Sticking.

She jumped up high
And smoothly
Landed back down into
Her partner's arms.

I think love is in the air
As they do their
Final jump, gracefully
Flying, twirling and
Landing.

Beth Sproston (9)
All Saints CE First School, Morpeth

Ice Skating In The Olympics

Sliding, graceful, colourful, ice, shiny, loving,
Fancy dresses, fun, jumpy, easy for some people,
Smooth and uplifting.

Exciting, flippy, floaty, smooth, skating, funny,
Fun and sometimes loving, caring and lovely.
Falling sadly in failure, splitting legs,
Hurting her knee, she is crying and sobbing,
With freezing arms,
Never doing ice skating again.

Alexandra Durance (9)
All Saints CE First School, Morpeth

Snowboarding

Here
He comes
The Flying Tomato,
Up he goes in the air
Tricks, turns, cool glides
And lots, lots more.

Snow-
Boarding's lots
Of fun and
I wish it was
The best I'd done.

Alison Russo (9)
All Saints CE First School, Morpeth

The Snowboard

The fast snowboard
Is very hard to master
While we have some pasta.

The spinning snowboard
In the cold air
While we have a pear.

The cold air of the snowboard
Soaring through the air
And down the mountain.

Curtis Jeffery (9)
All Saints CE First School, Morpeth

Ice Skating

The slippery, shiny ice frosting in the coldness,
Zipping across the soft, delicate ice.
She bounced and bobbed across the slidy ice.
She super-skidded across the ice and did some scary splits.
She got back on the white, slippery, frosty ice
To win the trophy.

Lauren Wigham (9)
All Saints CE First School, Morpeth

A Step In Life

With Barton School in front
And playgroup far behind
I cannot find the answers
To the questions in my mind.

Will I make new friends today
Or will I be alone?
I think I am going to have some fun
Before I set off home.

I have been here for a while now
And as happy as can be
September will be interesting
I am going to be Year 3.

I've like this place but now must go
It's time to say goodbye
Comberton is next for me
My biggest step in life.

Savannah Bennett (10)
Barton CE Primary School, Barton

The War

It was very scary, cos the war was going on,
People were yelling and crying for their sons.
Bullets hit the walls and firing was done,
It was very black and the sky was very dull.
Buildings were all wrecked, bombs were going off,
Houses always checked, sirens shouting out.
Helicopters flying, jets soaring through the air.
Lots of people dying, everyone was scared,
Years and years have passed, it has come to an end.

Andrew Healy (11)
Barton CE Primary School, Barton

Lucy

My dog Lucy was brown like chocolate.
My dog Lucy was small like a puppy.
My dog Lucy loved her treats.
My dog Lucy was thirteen.
My dog Lucy always played with me.
My dog Lucy was really lovely.
My dog Lucy loved her tea.
My dog Lucy had lots of fun.

My dog Lucy, gone, dead!

Amy Wilkins (10)
Barton CE Primary School, Barton

How To Make A Wishing Lake

First, dig a big hole with a pole,
Second, put in the water to stop human slaughter,
Third, get some fish to make a wish,
Fourth, make a wish in the very big dish
And before you know it, you will be a poet.

Georgia Smith (10)
Barton CE Primary School, Barton

Under The Sea

On the beach,
In the sand,
Under the water,
Dangerous creatures are landing on land.

What do we call these dangerous animals?
They're hippopotamus eels.
These animals are impossible
Because they're impossible to see,
That's why these animals
Should be under the sea.

Cally Saul (9)
Barton CE Primary School, Barton

Pants

Yellow pants, green pants,
Sometimes I wonder pants,
Everyday pants, new pants,
Old like a screw pants,
I wonder why, I wonder why,
Why have I got glue pants?
All around me everywhere
I've got pants, circle and square.

Toni Hardy (9)
Barton CE Primary School, Barton

Wayne Rooney

There was a footballer called Wayne,
He was a right old pain,
He played for Man U,
Everyone said, '*Boo!*'
He left on the London train.

Matthew Ellis (11)
Barton CE Primary School, Barton

Seasons

S ophie's garden is such a sight
P ansies are colourful
R uth is picking some flowers
I like green trees
N icola likes flowers
G ardening is fun.

S he is having an ice cream
U nder the beach umbrella
M um buys us an ice cream
M att plays beach ball
E mily swims in the sea
R ebecca is having fun.

A ll the leaves are turning brown
U mbrellas blow away on windy days
T rees are looking dull
U p the dark brown tree
M y plants are looking brown
N ick is making a leaf pile.

W illiam builds snowmen
I like playing in the snow
N igel is playing in the snow with me
T homas is feeling chilly
E veline is having fun in the snow
R yan throws snowballs.

Sophie Bates (9)
Barton CE Primary School, Barton

Cats

Fat cats, thin cats, in-between cats,
Fat cats sit on mats,
While thin cats go after mice, how nice,
While in-between cats have fun eating a bun.
Oh, what fun to be a cat.
Just like that in a flash, like I'm gone in a dash.

Rebecca Woor (10)
Barton CE Primary School, Barton

People Dying

I am scared in my room,
Can you guess what's going on?
People are screaming, 'Dead!'
Another one gone.
The RAF getting closer to death.
A bad thing is beginning, everyone is crying.
More people are dying.
I saw my dad dead in front of me,
Dead as could be.
That night I was scared as I could be.
In a fight, a bullet went through me.
All the planes crashing, fires rising,
Bang! Ashes flying,
Suddenly everything was quiet.
Guess what?
Another riot.
By now I was hurt.
Still carrying a dead body up the hill,
Carrying a dead body up the hill.
It was the pilot, his name was Bill.
Now I didn't care,
No more! No more! No more!

Joel Saul (13)
Barton CE Primary School, Barton

The Eagle

Today a battle, tomorrow a victory.
The pounding of drums and bayonets twirling,
The roaring of cannons and the blinding of powder.

A French column charging from the smoking powder,
Chanting 'Vive la France' to their sergeant major.
There we stood, shivering in fear,
Looking dead centre where an eagle-bearer walked,
Get it we must, 'Three rounds a minute,' our major said.

James Prince (9)
Barton CE Primary School, Barton

Warfare

It began.
Booms screeching above my head
Wish I was in my bed
Lights flashing in the air
People dying everywhere
Why, why, why did this start?
Bullets faster than a dart
Other side winning, winning war
I can hear my children at my bedroom door
Time going like a clock
A bullet hits me, what a shock
All around people dying
When a bomb hits them they go flying
I get to the turret and mount my gun
When I shoot a guy my mission is done
Soon after, in the air, the RAF is there
I have a better look with my sniper
Then I am bitten by a viper
Oh no! I am dying
The viper's bite is hypnotizing
I am wondering where the viper came from
After that my friend is gone, *no!*
I scream, my friend is dead.

Alan Hall (10)
Barton CE Primary School, Barton

Tornado!

Everyone is running
Shouting like mad
I can't believe it's happening
I'm beginning to blame Dad
I don't know how it started
Or even why
But I know I won't survive
So bye!

Abigail Johnson (10)
Barton CE Primary School, Barton

The Seasons Of A Flower

Spring:
There's blossom on the trees
And I'm just a little seed
Waiting to grow big and bright.

Summer:
There are many, many leaves on my stem now
The sun is warming my petals
And the rain is dampening the soil
Bees and other insects are flying and crawling all around.

Autumn:
The leaves on the trees are golden
And some are falling to the ground
I'm probably the brightest plant all around for miles.

Winter:
The trees are bare
And I'm no longer big and bright
My petals have fallen off
And I think it's time to sleep
Until it's springtime again.

Sarah Pedder (10)
Barton CE Primary School, Barton

Butterflies

Spring brings	*b*	eautiful butterflies
Cooling	*u*	nder trees
Leave	*t*	hem be under trees
Laying eggs	*t*	here on a leaf
Soon	*e*	merge the creepy caterpillars
Then a cool ch	*r*	ysalis hatching
Time to	*f*	ly
Butterf	*l*	y
Flutter b	*y*.	

Emma Bithell (9)
Barton CE Primary School, Barton

Black Cloud

The black raincloud drifts across the sky
Like a sheet of death,
Like a scene from Macbeth
Throwing rain over the unsuspecting victims,
Filling the seas, watering the crops
And annoying the townsfolk.
Suddenly the bright sun comes,
As if from nowhere,
Freeing the town's people from their homes.
Playing in the park, cycling on the road,
Suddenly, *black cloud*.
It comes again like a stabbing in the sky.
Everyone runs inside for shelter,
The televisions turn on.
Black cloud.

Ryan Chamberlain-Cox (11)
Barton CE Primary School, Barton

Big Bang, Big Wars

Big bangs,
Big booms,
Big wars,
Big war vehicles,
Big tragedy,
Big war zones,
No peace,
No love,
Lots of bombed homes and schools,
No one in town
There is no town.

Josh Nathan (11)
Barton CE Primary School, Barton

Who Can I Trust?

My name is Katy from Bangladesh,
Who can I trust when the world is at rest?
I've never feared an eagle,
I've never loved the sun,
I only know of ducks and of fun,
Still who can I trust?

Can I trust Rocky?
Can I trust Fred?
Maybe it's something,
I just don't know
What to do?
Who to tell?
Please, someone somewhere spill.

I've never heard of apple pies,
Only ever of spies and chives.
Explosives and bombs don't sound uncommon,
Can I trust the people who tell me of blossom?
Maybe I can't.
Who knows?

Sophie Martin (11)
Barton CE Primary School, Barton

The Gymawocky Poem
(Based on 'Jabberwocky' by Lewis Carroll)

'Twas time and the crowd roared
Did shout and cheer in the arena;
All enthusiastic were the gymnasts,
And the young girl elegantly entered.

'Beware the Redbridge Lions, my girl!
The jaws that bite, the claws that catch,
Beware the Albany Birds and shun
The Dako Angels!'

She took her gymnastic ribbon in hand
Long time the somersaulting foe she sought
So rested she by the beam tree,
And stood awhile in thought.

And as in headstand thought she stood,
The Spartack with eyes of flame
Came cartwheeling through the gymnastic team
And bringing completion as they came.

One, two! One, two! And through and through,
The dreaded vault came up,
She went with dread and with her legs,
She flipped and handsprung back.

'And hast thou slain the golden medal?
Come to my arms my beam-ish girl,
Oh balanced day, stay stay,
The audience chortled in joy.

'Twas time and the crowd roared
Did shout and cheer in the arena,
All enthusiastic were the gymnasts
And the young girl elegantly left.

**Sarah Wingett, Rebecca Millward, Emily Grimes (11)
& Abbie Schafer (10)**
Benhurst Primary School, Hornchurch

Doctorwocky
(Based on 'Jabberwocky' by Lewis Carroll)

'Twas blue, and the light on the top,
Did flash and sparkle in the street.
All adventurous was the Doctor
And the beautiful Rose Tyler.

'Beware the golden Daleks, my son!
The gun that shoots, the laser that kills.
Beware Cassandra, the skin on the rack
And shun the mighty Jagrafess!'

He took his sonic screwdriver in hand,
A long time the Doctor's foe he sought,
So rested he by the travelling tree
And stood awhile in thought.

And, as he stood too nervous to fight,
The werewolf, claws or razors
Came racing through the old monster wood
And killing as it came.

One, two, one, two, and through and through,
The lasered screwdriver went *buzz, buzz, buzz.*
The Doctor left it dead, and with its head,
He went on proudly back.

'And hast thou slain the mighty werewolf?
Come and give me a hug, the best Doctor!
O wonderful day, hip hip hooray,'
Rose chortled in her joy.

'Twas blue, and the light on the top,
Did flash and sparkle in the street.
All adventurous was the Doctor
And the beautiful Rose Tyler.

Emma Askew, Joshua Birch (10) & Ellen Glazebrook (9)
Benhurst Primary School, Hornchurch

Choccywocky

(Based on 'Jabberwocky' by Lewis Carroll)

'Twas frothy and the toffee
Did harden in my mouth
All chewy was the strawberry gum
And soon one tooth fell out!

'Beware the choccywocky my girl
The chocolate that melts, the hunger in its eyes
Beware the health bird and eat the
Chocolate giant!'

She took her Galaxy bar in hand
Long time the milky foe she sought
So rested her by the bubble gum tree
And stood awhile in thought.

And as in chocolatey thought she stood
The choccywocky with eyes of Skittles
Came bubbling through the candy wood
Eating as it came.

One, two! One, two! And through and through
The candy blade went *swish, swoosh!*
She left it dead and with its head
She went on skipping back.

'And hast thou killed the choccywocky?
Come to my arms my candy girl!
O Galaxy day! Hooray! Hooray!'
She giggled in her joy.

'Twas frothy and the toffee
Did harden in my mouth
All chewy was the strawberry gum
And soon one tooth fell out.

Emma Hankin (10) & Eva Ahern (9)
Benhurst Primary School, Hornchurch

Gobblerwocky
(Based on 'Jabberwocky' by Lewis Carroll)

'Twas sizzling and the succulent sausages
Did spit and hiss in the lard
All fluffy were the Yorkshires
And the gravy stood guard

'Beware the stinky Stilton cheese man, my son!
The claws that catch, the jaws that bite
And the Capt'n Birds Eye and shun,
The wobbly jelly'

He took his candy cane in hand
Long time the mouldy foe he sought
So rested he by the round trees
And stood awhile in thought

And, as in spaghetti thought he stood
The stinky Stilton cheese man
With eyes of peas,
Came gobbling through the macaroni wood
And burped as it came

One, two! One, two! And through and through
The candy cane went snickers snack
He left it dead and with its head
He went citrusing back

'And hast thou slain the stinky Stilton cheese man?
Come to my arms, my sweet boy
O meringue day, calamari! Caramel!'

'Twas sizzling and the succulent sausages
Did spit and hiss in the lard
All fluffy were the Yorkshires
And the gravy stood guard.

Rosie Wallace, Lucy Austin (10) & Hannah Clements (9)
Benhurst Primary School, Hornchurch

Doggiewocky
(Based on 'Jabberwocky' by Lewis Carroll)

'Twas hairy and the cute bulldog
Did run and play in the park
All fluffy were the puppies
And the Norfolk terrier yapped and barked.

'Beware the fearsome Argente rabbit, my boy,
The jaws that bite, the claws that catch,
Beware the husky and shun
The golden retriever.'

He took his marrow bone in mouth,
Long time the neighbour's rabbit foe he sought -
So rested he by the water bowl
And lay awhile in thought.

And as in deep thought he lay,
The speedy rabbit with shiny fur
Came bouncing through the leafy garden,
Eating the grass as it came.

One, two! One, two! And through and through!
The marrow bone went *crash!* and *bang!*
And he left it dead and with its head
He went on toddling back.

'And hast thou killed the Argente rabbit?
Come to my arms, my clever dog,
O marvellous day! Hooray! Hoorah!'
He chortled in his joy!

'Twas hairy and the cute bulldog
Did run and play in the park,
All fluffy were the puppies
And the Norfolk terrier yapped and barked.

Amy Johns & Molly Tyler (11)
Benhurst Primary School, Hornchurch

Chewywocky
(Based on 'Jabberwocky' by Lewis Carroll)

'Twas brilliant and the everlasting gum
Did slop and slop in the shop
All chewy were the chewy gums
And the children turned red with sour gums

'Beware the sneaky Snicker my son
The jaws that bite, the claws that catch
Beware the crunchy Malteser bird and shun
The Smartie eagle'

He took his chompy sword in hand
Long time the sneaky Snicker foe he sought
So rested by the chewy tree
And stood awhile in thought

And as in chewy candy thought he stood
The sneaky Snicker with eyes of flame
Came sneaking through the candy wood

One, two, one two, and through and through
The chompy sword went searing
He left it dead and with its head
He went eating his sword back

'And hast thou slain the sneaky Snicker
Come to my arms my candy boy
O chewy day! Yum-yum! Hooray!'

'Twas brilliant and the everlasting gum
Did slop and slop in the shop
All chewy were the chewy gums
And the children turned red with sour gums.

Joe Groves & Liam Mercer (10)
Benhurst Primary School, Hornchurch

Sportywocky
(Based on 'Jabberwocky' by Lewis Carroll)

'Twas scoring and football
Did kick and save in the hall
All bouncy were the basketballs
And the swimming is taught

'Beware the Sportywocky, my son
The balls that roll, the racket that hits
Beware the netball lovers, and shun
The cricket losers!'

He took his powerful racket in hand
Long time the games were finished
So rested he by the goalpost
And stood awhile in thought

And all as in golf he thought he stood
The Sportywocky with eyes like balls
Came kicking through the sports wood
And whacked the golf balls as it came

One, two, one, two, and through and through
The powerful bat went through it
He left it dead and with its head
He went on racing back

'And hast thou slain the Sportywocky
Come to my arms my sporty boy
O World Cup day, score, score, hooray'
He chortled in his joy

'Twas scoring and football
Did kick and save in the hall
All bouncy were the basketballs
And the swimming is taught.

Alexandra Georgiou (10)
Benhurst Primary School, Hornchurch

Schoolywocky
(Based on 'Jabberwocky' by Lewis Carroll)

'Twas playtime and the boys roared,
Did Mr and Mrs Talk in the staffroom,
All the bullies were in trouble
And the rest were indoors.

'Beware the Ebele brains, my son,
The leaky pens, the sharp pencils,
Beware the Monday morning assemblies,
And shun the hymn practice.'

He took his cricket bat in hand,
Long time the cricket ball foe he sought,
So rested he by the blueberry tree
And stood awhile in boredom.

And as in deep boredom he stood,
The Ebele, with eyes of flame,
Came running through the noisy playground
And swiped his bat as he came.

One, two! One, two! And through and through,
The wooden bat went into Ebele,
He left her dead and with her head,
He went to Mr Hobson.

'And hast thou slain the Ebele,
Come to my arms, my son.
O brilliant day! Hip hip hooray!'
He chortled in his joy!

'Twas playtime and the boys roared,
Did Mr and Mrs Talk in the staffroom,
All bullies were in trouble
And the rest were indoors.

Joe Kavanagh & Joe Williams (10)
Benhurst Primary School, Hornchurch

Brocciwocky
(Based on 'Jabberwocky' by Lewis Carroll)

'Twas tasty and the sausages,
Did sizzle and spit in the pan,
All slippery was the spaghetti
And the drink refreshing from the can.

'Beware the Brocciwock, my son!
The killer bite, the jaws and claws,
Beware the Brussels sprouts and shun,
The tasteless, horrid paw-paw!'

He took his vegetable knife in hand,
Long time the revolting foe he sought,
So rested he by the bubblegum tree
And stood awhile in thought.

And as in hungry thought he stood,
The Brocciwork, with eyes of flame,
Came hopping through the threatening forest
And killing things as it came.

One, two! One, two! And through and through,
The veggie blade went *chop, chop!*
He left it dead and with its head,
He went to his father's shop.

'And hast thou slain the Brocciwock?
Come to my arms, my bold, brave boy!
O glorious day! Hooray! Hooray!'
He chortled in his joy.

'Twas tasty and the sausages,
Did sizzle and spit in the pan,
All slippery was the spaghetti
And the drink refreshing from the can.

Ebele Nwangwu & Bethany Humphrey (11)
Benhurst Primary School, Hornchurch

What Has Happened To Mother, Daddy?

What has happened to Mother, Daddy?
We miss her shepherd's pie,
Is she in your wardrobe, Daddy,
With your best black tie?

Why are you crying, Daddy?
Please tell us why.
Is she in a hot air balloon, Daddy,
Flying really high?

Why are you looking at her picture, Daddy?
We need some new shoes.
Is she on a shopping spree, Daddy,
Getting all the gossip and news?

Is she adopting a sister for us, Daddy,
Or has she got the flu?
Are you getting divorced, Daddy?
Please tell us it's not true.

Well, my sweet, lovely cup cakes,
It's awfully hard to tell you.
Mother and I are getting divorced,
But we will always love you.

Sophie Childerhouse & Kayleigh Watts (10)
Blackdale County Middle School, Norwich

My Sister

I saw her, I saw her, I saw her cry
With the gleaming, glistening tear in her eye.
I watched her support system while it was on
Heard the worrying sound of Mother hum.
The nurse came in and she said,
'If we don't do something, she'll be dead.'
I hugged Mother as she wept,
Watched my sister as she slept.
Worries swam round my head,
If we don't do something she'll be dead.
I watched Mother put Teddy in her arms,
I squeezed her hand and stroked her palm.
She was cold. No! It couldn't be.
Please, sister, don't die on me.

Danielle Haycock (10)
Blackdale County Middle School, Norwich

What's The Rabbit Doing Mum?

What's the rabbit doing Mum?
What will he have to eat?
Will he have an apple
For a special treat?

Will he be alright Mum?
I hope he doesn't die.
Don't worry, dear, don't fret yourself,
I think he will survive.

We'll keep an eye on it,
We'll visit every day,
We'll make sure he's safe and well
And keep him here to stay.

Marcus Kerton & Ross Schuller (10)
Blackdale County Middle School, Norwich

Bear In A Cage

When I went on a trip for a treat,
I saw a bear in a cage.
I looked in the eyes of the bear
And saw they were full of rage.

Badly treated on a bear farm,
They stuck needles through her fur,
To take things to make medicine,
Not caring if it hurt.

I felt this wasn't fair,
I sighed and I felt sad.
Mum didn't seem to care and said,
'Don't let it make you feel bad.

Don't let it ruin your trip,
What else do you want to see?'
I didn't answer, I just ran
And set the poor bear free.

Bethany Chapman (10)
Blackdale County Middle School, Norwich

My Cousin Ran Away

I once saw my cousin cry
I couldn't understand why
Then she left, she ran away
When I thought she'd come to stay.

My mother telephoned my aunt
Who said to her, 'I really can't
Imagine what has happened to her,
I wish her back, the way we were.'

Some time later she returned
With some money she had earned
'I'm happy now,' she sobbed and sniffed
'So happy I can buy a gift.'

Sophie Aldous & Jessica Chester (9)
Blackdale County Middle School, Norwich

Advice

Here is some advice . . .
    Have an argument with Arthur,
    Have a fight with Fred,
    Bickering with Bernie is quite amusing,
    But whatever you do,
    Never have a squabble with Spencer.

Imogen Mintram (10)
Blakesley CE Primary School, Blakesley

Trolls

Trolls, trolls, wonderful trolls,
They really love sausage rolls!
They are very big,
They love to play tig,
Whether it's rainy or dry.

Trolls, trolls, big fat trolls,
They love to cuddle little dolls,
Whether they're happy or sad,
I love trolls!

Beth Mintram (10)
Blakesley CE Primary School, Blakesley

Dolphins

Dolphins swimming in the aqua-blue
Swimming, splashing and playing too
You can swim with them
Feed them, talk to them too
Dolphins are wonderful creatures
Swimming in the aqua-blue.

Abigail Chambers (10)
Blakesley CE Primary School, Blakesley

School

S cary teachers shouting at us
C olourful dragons stuck on the wall
H elp! We're trapped in the classroom
O h no! I forgot my sick note, it's Wednesday!
O ur teacher, Mrs Henson, bites on Wednesday
L essons are so boring, they seem like a year long.

Charles Getter (10)
Blakesley CE Primary School, Blakesley

Dolphins

D ancing dolphins under the sea
O ver and over, over the waves
L ying on the seabed after being killed
P laying under the sea with their friends
H iding behind the sea plants
I n the warm sea having lots of fun
N ever rest, just keep going
S wimming in rings with their family.

Ryan Gyles (10)
Blakesley CE Primary School, Blakesley

A Gardener Kennings

A plant lover
A fork pusher
A spade heaver
A rabbit hater
A leaf composter
A bush cutter
A weed puller
A soil shoveller.

Ben Wright (10)
Brilley CE School, Whitney

Vegetable Gardener Kennings

A pest controller
A seed planter
A carrot puller
A potato forker
A runner bean raiser
A pea pod picker
A tomato tickler
A cucumber collector.

Laura Wright (8)
Brilley CE School, Whitney

A Gardener Kennings

A fork thrower
A grass mower
A rake puller
A spade digger
A weed hoer
A hole poker
A leaf blower
A ladder climber.

Ethan Roberts (8)
Brilley CE School, Whitney

Tools Kennings

A spade digger
A lawn cutter
A hole poker
A weed hoer
A fork whacker
A can dripper
A compost shredder
A rotovator driver.

Jamie Jerman (9)
Brilley CE School, Whitney

The Fox Kennings

A hunt abominator
A chicken adorer
A hound escaper
A den constructor
A brush owner
A scent leaver
A cub carer
A ground tunneller.

Lister Morris (11)
Brilley CE School, Whitney

The Golden Eagle Kennings

A Scottish swooper
An orb extensioner
A talon terror
A nest assembler
A flesh stealer
A screech screamer
A feather interlocker
A sovereign poacher.

Hattie Roberts (10)
Brilley CE School, Whitney

A Gardener Kennings

A rotovator tusher
A plant lover
A rabbit discourager
A vegetable grower
A spud digger
A woodpecker feeder
A compost composter
A weed sprayer.

David Price (11)
Brilley CE School, Whitney

The Hedgehog Kennings

A garden visitor
A winter hibernator
A worm eater
A flea owner
A prickle grower
A leaf rummager
A snuffle grunter
A ball roller.

Ben Woolley (8)
Brilley CE School, Whitney

Tortoise Kennings

A neck wrinkler,
An eye winker,
A grass waddler,
A water paddler,
A leaf muncher,
A vegetable cruncher,
A shell possessor,
A dinosaur professor.

Lucinda Jones (11)
Brilley CE School, Whitney

Pig Kennings

A root gobbler
A straw sniffer
A muck roller
A corn eater
A snout smeller
A field walker
A figure bristler.

Amy Griffiths (11)
Brilley CE School, Whitney

Swimming Pool

People splashing around in the swimming pool
Diving from great heights into the water
Splash!
The smell of chemicals from the water
Swishes around in the bottom of the swimming pool
Cold, dripping ice creams melting down the cone
It's so cold I get a brain freeze.
I'm feeling wavy like the splashing swimming pool.

Amber Glaysher (9)
Buxton CP School, Norwich

Hayden And The Chocolate Factory

Chocolate, different shapes and sizes,
Chocolate fountains too,
It's just too good,
For less than one day,
It's so lovely,
I wish I could come again.

Hayden Ramm
Buxton CP School, Norwich

Goal!

The ref blows his whistle
Whoo, whoo!
We are off,
Like horses coming out of the blocks.
The atmosphere is electric,
So good you can nearly smell it.
The tackle goes in, *crunch!*
We're on the break
And it's a *goal!*

Daniel Rivett (10)
Buxton CP School, Norwich

Death

Life is moving
The memories are coming back
More stress is here to haunt
Bombs are firing
Bullets are flying.

The morning glistens
The air is colder
It's not like home
You can hear
The guns
In the background.

People shouting
Nurses crying
It's here
Creeping around everything in sight
It leaves nothing behind.

It's closer
I can feel it
It's getting worse
I fear it's here.

Jake Webster
Buxton CP School, Norwich

The Beach

Beating down on the beach
As hot as hot can be
The people are peeking in
The windows of mermaids' houses
Sandcastles being built with care
Until the sea is hungry
Young ones playing 'it' with the sea
Lots of kids dropping sandwiches and ice creams
Kids crying because they have to go home
And leave this magical place
Then there is silence
Long silence
Not a sound
Until the sun comes up
Whoosh
Hundreds of people appear
It all happens again.

Megan Taylor (9)
Buxton CP School, Norwich

Beaches

I see the gentle waves,
Flowing softly.
Then I see a fisherman on his own,
Flick!
A fish flaps, dying in the boat.
I pick up a handful of soft sand
And dip it in and out of the sea.
The outside is wet,
But the inside is still soft.
I walk away, then turn my back
And see a sandcastle melt in the sea.

Taylor de Lucchi (9)
Buxton CP School, Norwich

The Football Ground

Turn up at the football ground
And you will hear some sounds
Especially the music
And the joke about Mick!

The ref blows his whistle, the game is underway!
All the supporters shout a giant *hooray!*
Half an hour later the game still tied
The forward gets tripped and starts to fly
The keeper's off, he's got a red
The forward's got a sore head!

'Goal!' shout the crowd, the ball's in the net
'Great!' yells John. 'I've won my bet!'
The whistle's gone, it's half-time
All the fans are eating pies!

The message I must now send
Is that this poem has come to an end!

Jamie Barnes (10)
Buxton CP School, Norwich

Farm

Farms are fun, farms are great
They're better than any other place
Smell the spring air
I taste pork sausages
I see pigs everywhere
Isn't it the best place to be?
Farms are fun
Farms are great
Why don't you come again?

Adam Gray (10)
Buxton CP School, Norwich

The Theme Park

Screaming and shouting fills the air
Hooray, hooray, we're at the fair
Everyone is having lots of fun
But all the babies do is suck their thumbs.

People queuing for bumper cars
Lots of eating at burger bars
Roller coaster goes very fast
Mum and Dad wave as it goes past.

Lots of people eating a meal
Children go on the Ferris wheel
Mum and Dad are getting cross
They're buying too much candyfloss.

It is the end of the day
All the staff shout, 'Hooray!'

Joshua Overton (10)
Buxton CP School, Norwich

Chip Shop

Tick-tock, tick-tock,
Chip-chop, chip-chop,
At the chip shop,
First come, first served,
Red sauce, brown sauce,
Sizzle, sizzle,
Splash, splash, splash,
Salt and vinegar,
Menus, adverts,
Chip-chop, chip-chop,
Tick-tock, tick-tock.

Chloe Gowen (10)
Buxton CP School, Norwich

I'm The Tree!

Wispy fingers,
Old, gnarled skin,
Old or young,
Fat or thin.

Straight or bent,
Bare or green,
Ageing, growing,
But never seen.

On its own,
Or in a crowd,
Showcased by moonlight,
Shadowed by cloud.

Always shouting,
'Look at me,
But look at me,
Old, gnarled and wispy,
I'm the tree!'

Katharine Butchers (10)
Buxton CP School, Norwich

The Match

Footie, footie, it's so exciting,
The stadium has lovely food and drink,
One goal, two goals, three goals, four,
I hope my team will score.
Even better front row seats,
Really happy and overjoyed,
Sitting with family and friends,
Everybody screaming and chanting too.
Oh, they are going, they are going . . .
Goal! Goal! Yes, we scored!

Tom Booth (9)
Buxton CP School, Norwich

At The Beach

People running round and round,
Children screaming all around,
Sand sizzles with the sun,
Children whizzing, sandcastles done.
Waves creeping up and down,
Sea salting, ice creams dropping.
Candy smelling, waves whooshing,
Children screaming, children running,
All at the beach.

Emma Waller (9)
Buxton CP School, Norwich

The Take-Away

Hungry
Hungry
The smells are overwhelming me
I have to have it
I must
I have the money in my hands
I just need it
Need it
Sizzle
Crackle
Pop
I must
I must
I must
I can't stand it anymore
Finally, tastes delicious
Better than I've dreamt it to be.

James Douglas
Buxton CP School, Norwich

Roller Coaster

Rides whizzing, music playing,
People running to go on a ride.
Kids eating too much candyfloss.
Hundreds of people in every queue,
One ride broken, one ride fixed.
Everyone rushing to that line.
One ride red, one ride yellow and blue.
Burgers going with the drinks.
Some people leaving, more people coming.
Nobody cares, they just want to get here first!
People going to the gift shop to remind them of the day.

Harry Dread
Buxton CP School, Norwich

Mr Martin

Mr Martin is my teacher,
He really acts like a mythical creature.

He shouts and also makes us laugh,
With his shirt as white as a cloud.

He is rather scary and
He eats lots of dairy (chocolates!).

He catches people,
Keeps us in.

When my teacher's hair goes up,
I know it is because of the wind.

Paris Demetriou (9)
Chesterfield Junior School, Enfield

Symptoms Of A Winter

Tonight the brittle trees,
Vigorously dive in all directions at once.
Their skeletal bodies
Reaching over to grab the ground to hold themselves down.

The wind whistles
A sad, mournful tune, made up of a few notes.
It drags along the few things
That don't keep themselves upright.

The curtains of rooms,
Billow inwards, like a child trying to keep a secret,
Until finally,
In one great gust of wind, they let it all out.

Small breaths of cold
Creep into the warm, firelit home,
Like a spy on a secret mission,
It is a well-trained spy, for it fails to be noticed.

Blankets of soft, white snow,
Have been draped over every possible surface,
A silky coat
That only the sun can move.

Then the end of the day comes,
Just as quickly as the last one went.
Another day has passed
And still winter keeps its cold.

Maddy Richardson (11)
City of London School for Girls, London

Witch's Spell

When the battle is in distress,
With a little trickiness,
Cooking some roasted stew
Which holds a disgusting brew?

The heart will always see the crime
Which lies buried within time,
When it's transparent to the eye
And time will prove that truth does lie
And words to blind us to our dreams
And nothing's ever what it seems,
And nothing can be what it's not,
This then is on the fated plot.
Everyone takes out the code,
When people are on this deepest road!

Mustafa C Kherbane (9)
Harlesden Primary School, London

Recipe For Disaster

Make, make, bake a cake
Right now there's no mistake.

Eye of newt and toe of frog,
Wool of bat and tongue of dog,
Fire of dragon and brain of lion,
Claw of crow and breath from the dying,
Tail of cow,
To make it right now!
Paw of rabbit,
Nose of hobbit,
Skin of hen
And straw from a den.
Mix it up, what do you make?
A witch's wicked cauldron cake!

Sokaina Zaari (9)
Harlesden Primary School, London

Witch's Spell

(Inspired by 'Macbeth' by William Shakespeare)

Double, double, toil and trouble,
Let smoke burn and cauldron bubble.

Eye of bird and tongue of snake,
In a cauldron grill and bake.
Liver of lizard and head of cat,
Leg of horse and tail of rat,
Vampire fang and wing of bat.
For a charm to cause powerful trouble,
Just like Hell-broth and bubble!

Mital Pratap (9)
Harlesden Primary School, London

Witch's Spell

Double, double, boil and trouble,
Let fire burn and cauldron bubble.

Tongue of frog
And tail of dog,
In the cauldron boil and bubble,
This really means double trouble.

Grilled eye of newt
And a really smelly boot.
Dripping tears of bat
And the heart of a cat.
Ear of deer
And some sickly beer.

For a charm that will harm,
You will wake up in alarm!

Abdikafi Dahir (9)
Harlesden Primary School, London

Witch's Spell

Shimmer, shimmer, simmer and simmer,
Fire burn and cauldron glimmer.
Eye of bat and body of snake,
In the cauldron fry and bake.
Fire boiling full with trouble,
Bubble, bubble, toil and bubble.
Eye of frog,
Hair of dog,
The witch's spell will make you shudder
When bat's blood makes you another.

Anam Parveen (8)
Harlesden Primary School, London

Witch's Spell

Double, double, rock and rumble,
Fire burn and cauldron bubble.

Eye of bat and tongue of snake,
In the cauldron fry and bake.

Pig's heart, tiger's tail,
Lizard's leg, frog's nail.

This will create a wicked feast,
To turn the gentle to a beast!

Jay Pratap (9)
Harlesden Primary School, London

Witch's Spell

Fiddle, riddle, boil and sizzle,
Fire burn and cauldron frizzle.

Fillet of a bat
That looks like a cat.
Eyes of a dog,
A frog from a log
And bird flu
Is coming to you!
Mix it up and you will find,
This wicked brew will blow your mind!

Simon Fatimehin (9)
Harlesden Primary School, London

Witch's Spell

Double trouble, boil and bubble,
Smoke burn and fire trouble.

Rotten liver and dead man's cat,
Toe of toad and wing of bat,
Eye of frog and nose of newt,
Fin of a fish and smelly plant root,
Elephant's trunk and neck of beetle,
Tongue of lizard and blood like treacle,
For a crime of fury and fire,
Drink this broth to be a liar!

Alyah Sharifah Lewis (9)
Harlesden Primary School, London

Witch's Spell

A heart will always
Tell the crime
So drink the brew and be mine.

So you can always
Prove it all the time,
Come and chant the witch's rhyme,
Then when you start to dream,
Charms and chants will make you scream!

Nur Mohamed (9)
Harlesden Primary School, London

Witch's Spell

Fillet of dog and a smelly frog,
With a rat and a bat,
With blood from a cat,
Now you can drink my poisonous brew,
I will give you power too.
Place the locks from a boiled ox,
Grind up rocks with a grilled fox,
Place them in my magic pot,
You will become something you are not!

Anthony O'Connor (9)
Harlesden Primary School, London

The Nasty Broth!

Riddle, riddle, kill and fiddle,
Witch's brew put on a griddle.

Blend, chop and grate, leave to bake,
Cauldrons conjure up my cake.
Thigh of a dog and bloodthirsty bat,
Snake's rattle and a crazy cat.
Cow's brain cell and a hen's toenail,
Rat's tail, coming from the Royal Mail,
For a cake that casts a spell,
Eat this and you'll feel unwell!

Nikita Braithwaite & Anisa Abdul-Kadir (9)
Harlesden Primary School, London

Witch's Spell

Double, double, toil and trouble,
Fire burn and cauldron bubble.
Lizard leg and owl's wing,
For a charm that will sting.

Cat's legs and nose of dog,
Bat's wing and slimy frog.
Churn them up 'til they wail,
Slices of brain, a mouse's tail.

Ladana Mohamed Awil
Harlesden Primary School, London

Witch's Spell

Wobble, double, boil the trouble,
Black smoke burn and cauldron bubble.

Boil a girl with the name of Kate,
In the cauldron shake a snake.
Sweat of sock and eye of dog,
Brain of bat and hair of hog,
Cut toenail and cauldron bubble
And mouse tail from double trouble.

Sananthen Balaskander
Harlesden Primary School, London

Witch's Spell

Fire, fire, burn higher,
Toe of lizard, leg of frog,
Juice of beetle, tail of dog.

Fork of adder, burnt pig,
Grilled snakes from the digs.
Let the cauldron flow and rumble
And the witches moan and grumble.

Ryan Dolling (9)
Harlesden Primary School, London

Scary Spell

Cauldron, cauldrons give me power,
And magic me a poison flower.

Filthy oyster from its shell,
Place in the cauldron from Hell,
Make me a dish, from the fin of a fish
And grant me the magic of a powerful wish!

Julio Pashollari (9)
Harlesden Primary School, London

My Future

It would be a very nice place
If the world, in ten years or more, was the same.

Will the blue whale still swim in the silvery, lush seas?

It really would be a nice place if there was no gun crime or violence
And there was peace in the world.

Will there still be green grass for us to play on
And will there still be football pitches for the World Cup to be held?

Luke Simmons (8)
Keble Prep School, London

The Big Fir Tree

It is older than I am,
Eight years, ten months am I.
It stands like a pyramid
Or the perfect triangle.

It is wider than a truck,
But as thin as a rake on top.
It makes a noise like mumbling
In a school classroom.

It's taller than my house
And next door.
It's rough like the pebble-dashed wall,
With skin all brown and hard.

Its needles are as green as my army tank,
Its body is straight like a Roman soldier.
Its branches smell of the sweet scent
Of resinous sap.

Bolaji Anifalaje (8)
Keble Prep School, London

The Magic Box
(Based on 'Magic Box' by Kit Wright)

I will put in my box . . .
The screeching of monkeys in the tropical rainforest,
Bright-coloured birds flying in the peaceful sky,
A slithering snake gliding along the rough tree trunks.

I will put in my box . . .
A sky full of white clouds with silver sparkled angels,
A jumbo jet roaring through the clouds with a thunderbolt,
A flash of lightning blazing in the sky with a fiery spark.

I will put in my box . . .
An enormous wave rolling down onto the flat surface
With a gigantic splash,
A speedboat racing through the sea with jets of water
Shooting into the air,
The beautiful different coloured cord, yellow, red and purple.

I will put in my box . . .
A flying car with feathered wings,
An eagle driving along the motorway,
A mummified body on a blue cow.

My box is fashioned from marble and varnished wood,
It has sparkling diamonds on the lid
And gold bars on the bottom.
The handles are made from steel and iron.

I shall ski in my box on the high slopes of the Alps,
Along the winding piste
And come to rest tumbling down
Like a great big avalanche.

Nana Antwi (9)
Keble Prep School, London

My Future Poem

The world of my future is
Grey, brown and black:
Grey for concrete, brown for sky,
Black for darkness.
There was a war to end all wars,
That almost destroyed
Our world.
Many escaped to the safety of the underground,
We need food and water,
It is damp and dark underground.
We've been here years,
In this safety of the underground.
I think about outside,
The blue sky, green grass
Blowing in the wind,
The smell of fresh air,
All the things we do not have now.
I cannot stand being underground anymore.
I poke out my head.
The air smells dusty, the ground is rough.
Everywhere I look is dusty and grey,
The results of the terrible war.
But there in the distance
Is a little green shoot.
The memories of dark and dusty years
Will fade with the hope
That this one tiny shoot brings.

Rhys Beacham (8)
Keble Prep School, London

The War Of The Clouds

Cotton wool clouds,
Filling the empty sky,
Stopping the angry sun
From watching the world go by.

Beads of shiny silver,
The pearl-like drops of water,
Dancing in the festive clouds,
Making the ferocious sun feel hotter.

Raindrops are dancing fairies,
Flying down, towards the ground,
Turning everything they touch
Into pearls of different colours.

The clouds begin to vanish,
The sun admires the sparkles from the drops
Of pearls, that the fairies left behind,
Reflecting the golden rays of happiness.

Mohsin Abedi (9)
Keble Prep School, London

Clouds

It's a silky candyfloss,
It's a kettle's smoke,
It's a puff of dragon's smoke,
It's a reel of cotton wool.

It's a sailing ship,
It's a river of wind,
It's a cotton ball high up in the sky,
It's a wave flying through the air.

It's a gliding plane,
It's a puff of white water,
It's a choo-choo train,
It's God's footprint.

Tomi Badmos (9)
Keble Prep School, London

The Magic Box
(Based on 'Magic Box' by Kit Wright)

I will put in the box . . .
The strings of a smooth violin,
The sight of my baby brother when I first saw him,
The sight of a little rabbit and the first flower to grow in spring.

I will put in the box . . .
The warm sun on a sunny day
And the aroma of fresh air.

I will put in the box . . .
The smoothness of a skateboard's wheels
And the sound of a car getting ready to race.
The sound of a piano and the taste of pizza.
The smell of petrol and the roar from a giant.

My box is fashioned from ice that will never smash or melt.
I shall be as small as a mouse, so that I can fit in the box.

Adeniran Thompson (9)
Keble Prep School, London

My Magic Cloud

It's a fluffy piece of cotton wool,
It's a fish from McElliot's pool.

It's the froth from a tasty beer,
It's a big white mattress made in Korea.

It's an ice cream sundae,
It's a meringue made on Monday.

It's a big grey wig,
It's a blanket covering a pig.

It's a sleeping hippo in the sky,
It's a fluffy cushion way up high.

It's a huge, white, tragic crowd,
It's nothing but my magic cloud!

Charlie Pearch (9)
Keble Prep School, London

My Future

Will ivory still be hunted
Or will elephants become extinct?
I hope that all the poachers
Will all sit down and think.

Will there still be polluted oceans
Or will dolphins swim with ease?
I hope that all polluters
Will stop ruining our seas.

Will there still be global warming
Or will the ice caps melt away?
I hope this doesn't happen
I think I'll sit down and pray.

Will there still be wars and terrorists
Or will we destroy each other?
I hope that peace will prevail
And we'll all love one another.

Will I be a tinker, tailor or soldier
Or maybe I'll be famous and wealthy?
I don't really care, as long as I'm happy
And whatever will be will be.

Anthony Constantinou (9)
Keble Prep School, London

The Magic Box
(Based on 'Magic Box' by Kit Wright)

I will put in the box . . .
The first time I was whistling with Mum and Dad listening,
The first sight of my baby cousin,
The taste of an éclair.
I will put in the box . . .
The loudest heartbeat I've heard,
Untouched snow, crisp and while,
Pure orange juice, sweet to taste.
I will put in the box . . .
A crowd of laughing people,
An everlasting flame,
Freshly made pancakes.
I will put in the box . . .
A never-ending lollipop,
The scales of a dragon,
A wish to sail over the sea in the wind.
My box is fashioned from melted iron,
Decorated with eagles' feathers
And with the exoskeleton of a spider for a lock.
I shall fly in my box with angel's wings
And land in a giant tree house.

Sebastian Davis (8)
Keble Prep School, London

The Magic Box
(Based on 'Magic Box' by Kit Wright)

I will put in my holiday box . . .
The warm and rough feeling of sand between my toes in Barbados
The intoxicating smell of petrol from a gleaming white motorboat
The cackling of the seagulls piercing through the sky like a
                                                   sharp blade.

I will put in my wresting box . . .
The splash of scarlet blood dripping from the grey steel cage
The rippling, rough muscles of the wrestler, Battista
The Undertaker in the WWE makes me shiver like fish without water.

I will put in my rainbow-coloured box . . .
Red for dragons hotter than hot wax breath
Orange for quenching thirst
Yellow for the burning sun
Blue for the blue-scaled snake that slithers around the slopes
Indigo for the ink in the squid who lives in the Indian Ocean
Violet for the vile, vomiting vultures.

I will put in my magic sweets box . . .
Tongue-twisting twizzler tasting sweets
Super sour, sonic blasting swizzler
Big, blue, bubbly, balloon-blowing bubblegum.

My box is fashioned from diamonds, sapphires and rubies
With scales of the blue snake as a lid
And the arms of a wrestler as hinges.

Thomas Matthews (9)
Keble Prep School, London

My Future

What will the future be like?
Will the endangered animals be extinct
Or will they be safe?

Will pollution get worse
And make more disease
Or will our planet be green again?

Will our planet
Suffer enormous tsunamis bigger than now
Or will the ozone rebuild?

Will foods in the future
Have too much fat
Or will they be organic?

My future
Good or bad?
I would like good, for sure.

Will the sun be more powerful
And burn us to a crisp
Or will we be protected?
Just decide, good or bad for your future?

George Newton (8)
Keble Prep School, London

The Magic Box
(Based on 'Magic Box' by Kit Wright)

I will put in the box . . .
A firework exploding on a frosty night
A volcano erupting in a hot land
And a soft, furry rug to keep my feet warm.

I will put in the box . . .
Ice cream with a chocolate flake
A dolphin swishing with the waves
And a thunderbolt in the sky.

I will put in the box . . .
A hot, sunny Christmas Day
A footballer with ballet shoes
And money falling from the sky.

My box is fashioned from . . .
Diamonds and rubies
With silver glitter on the lid
And a keyhole.
When you open the box, books burst out.

I shall hide all the sweets in my box
Like a hungry lion satisfied with his feast.

Savvas Petrou (9)
Keble Prep School, London

The Magic Box
(Based on 'Magic Box' by Kit Wright)

I will put in the box . . .
A photo of the four of us having fun in Florida
A pencil which pongs of a papaya
A skateboard I use to slide down slippery slopes.

I will put in the box . . .
A brilliant white T-shirt
A sticky sweet toffee from Belgium
A screeching violin.

I will put in the box . . .
The velvety smoothness of a red rose
The twitter of a robin
And the chuckle of a baby.

I will put in my box . . .
An eighth day and a pink ocean
A cat that breathes fire
And a dragon that miaows.

My box is fashioned from chocolate and strawberries
With bubblegum on the lid and sweets in the corners.
Its hinges are liquorice sticks.
I shall fly in my box on a broomstick
Then land on the grass, surrounded by trees.

Bhavek Shah (9)
Keble Prep School, London

The Magic Box
(Based on 'Magic Box' by Kit Wright)

I will put in the box . . .
The susurration of rustling, serrated sycamore leaves,
A gigantic, galloping giraffe,
Grazing my knee on the gritty ground.

I will put in the box . . .
The crunching of cornflakes on the carpet,
The taste of a tangy tangerine,
The scorching sun in the summer sky.

I will put in the box . . .
A gargantuan, giggling, grotesque gargoyle,
The creaking of a castle door,
The big, bad bully's fist.

I will put in the box . . .
A third eye and a second mouth,
A knight in a spacesuit,
An astronaut in armour.

My box is fashioned from titanium and bronze
With crystal corners and a lapis lazuli lid.
The lock is made from a lion's claw.

I shall sleep in my box
And dream I am flying with pixies and elves
To a far-off forest,
Where I can play in jelly meadows and sherbet rivers.

Zachary Woodhouse (9)
Keble Prep School, London

Metaphor Poem About Clouds

It's a colossal black gorilla
It's a football match lost one-nil
It's a deadly red vampire
It's a monster about to kill

It's an ancient coat of grey
It's a break up with best friend
It's a soldier's march to war
It's a holiday come to an end

It's a Mayan temple in Citchen Itza
It's Statue of Liberty standing with grace
It's the endless Wall of China
It's the sphinx with a sandy face

It's a ballerina's fancy dress
It's candyfloss given to me
It's a scattering of autumn leaves
It's a blazing ball of fire, can't you see?

Henry Jeffery (9)
Keble Prep School, London

The Magic Box
(Based on 'Magic Box' by Kit Wright)

In my box I will put . . .
The swoosh of a snowboard on a winter night
And the smell of fresh air
The hum of a hummingbird.

In my box I will put . . .
The swoosh of the sea on a windy day
And the sound of a gallop from a horse
The sound of ripping paper on Christmas Day.

In my box I will put . . .
The feeling of snow on your cheek
The fresh taste of fish
The warmth of fire on your hands.

My box is made from steel and iron with horns on top.

Oliver Keane (9)
Keble Prep School, London

The Door
(Based on 'The Door' by Miroslav Holub)

Go and open the door,
Maybe outside there's a golden eagle
Swooping to and fro between the trees.

Go and open the door,
Maybe there's a big buffalo,
Charging at the red blankets blowing in the wind.

Go and open the door,
Maybe outside there's a black horse
Galloping around the smooth, green grass.

Connor Baird (8)
Langham Primary School, Langham

Winter?

Bobble-hatted children
Screams of delight
Jumping down the hill having snowball fights
But where's the snow?

Cotton wool covers the street
The snow is turning to sky
Blue sleet
Winter blowing in my face
But where's the snow?

Chunks of snowdrops smacking my face
Icy trees pointing to the silver sky
Children hiding
But where's the snow?

Pierce Rannigan (9)
Maldon Primary School, Maldon

Is This Winter?

I'm walking on frosted grass,
It's like the sound my mum hates.
Is this winter?
Frost lying on window ledges,
Like you've just sprinkled flour all over a cake.
Is this winter?
Vehicles and other objects that just sit around
Are covered with blankets that look like you've spilt glitter all over.
Frosted air everywhere, singing to you.
Is this winter?
Trees are wearing a cloak of cotton with branches poking you.
Snow is falling, so this is *winter*.

Amy Rolfe (9)
Maldon Primary School, Maldon

Where's The Snow?

Children with clothes as bright as stars at midnight,
Children sliding down all the pelted streets,
We don't want rafts of warm, delicious sunlight,
But where's the snow?

Freezing iced windscreens,
All coated cars stay in their place,
The cars and trucks are dressed in dazzling, glittery, white snow,
But where's the snow?

Perfectly round snowballs flying everywhere,
Snowboards going down steep, polished hills,
Skiers behind the boarders, everyone's having fun,
But where's the snow?

Doors frozen shut by muscled ice,
Icicles as sharp as razors hanging from all the houses,
People drinking hot chocolate, as hot as lava,
Here's the snow!

Jake Gilroy (8)
Maldon Primary School, Maldon

Where's Winter?

The children playing in scarves and hats,
Leaving footprints in the deep, cotton wool-like snow,
Making beautiful snow angels.
But where's winter?
Cars creeping past on the polished, icy roads,
Soft snow falling on the cars like sugar lumps,
Cars getting buried in snow.
But where's winter?
Mysterious birds leaving footprints,
Icicles hanging off trees.
Next day, wake up very early, get ready to play,
Winter is here.

Bethany Williams (8)
Maldon Primary School, Maldon

But Where's The Snow?

Piles of snow
Like trenches which cars go through.
Iced-up cars.
But where's the snow?

Layers of thick white snow
Like Jack had killed grass with it.
But where's the snow?

Snow flopping on the ground
Like Jack dropping snowballs down.
But where's the snow?

Powerful wind directing the snow.
But where's the snow?

People put on coats, hats and gloves.
Happy snowmen.
Here's the snow.

Joel Manning (9)
Maldon Primary School, Maldon

Winter?

Icy rain zooming from the sky
Gales of wind blows trees down
Cold weather hits the Earth
But when's the snow coming?
Fields get smothered in frost
Puddles turn into ice
Rain turns into hailstones smashing to the ground
But when is the snow coming?
One morning a snowflake falls
Like a grain of sand.
When is the snow coming?
Now!

Ashley Green (8)
Maldon Primary School, Maldon

Winter

Blankets of snow cover the vehicles all across the street,
Footprints big and small, snaking across the ice,
Beautiful snow angels clear the snow.

                                          (But where's the snow?)

Trees covered with white ice,
Ice frozen around the leaves,
Making leaves drop.

                                          (But where's the snow?)

The ground is like mountains of snow,
It heaps the cars.

                                          (But where's the snow?)

Thursday, February 22nd,
It's cold outside.
Here's the snow.

Amie Bridge (8)
Maldon Primary School, Maldon

Winter Days

Children wrapped up in woolly scarves, gloves and hats.
The trees look like they are putting on their robes of snow
And shaking off their cloaks of leaves.
The grass is frozen where it stands.
Jack Frost has painted the pavements and the roads.
The rooftops are covered in a snowy massacre,
The cars are in the middle of a snowy blizzard.
People in shops buying presents for Christmas.
Birds chirping, but you can't see them.
Windscreens of cars covered in icy snow.
Gales of wind hit the ground,
Hailstones falling from the sky, hitting children.
The rain pelting down to earth trying to make things better,
But it makes it worse.

Calum Banks (9)
Maldon Primary School, Maldon

Winter?

Ice-coated windscreens,
Frosted air,
Frozen lakes,
                        But where's the snow?

Frozen windows everywhere,
Heaps of wadding,
Snow angels made by children,
                        But where's the snow?

Snowballs flying everywhere,
Sledges going downhill,
Icy trees pointing to the silver sky,
                        But where's the snow?

Thursday, 23rd February,
Here's the snow!

Thomas Parmenter (9)
Maldon Primary School, Maldon

Is This Winter?

Deep, deep snow that comes up to your knees,
Millions of snowflakes that glide in the breeze,
Child-sized snow angels spread on the ground,
         But is this winter?
Frozen lakes so you can ice skate,
Snowmen watching people snow fight,
Muffled-up children scurrying like ants,
         But is this winter?
Icicles hanging as sharp as knives,
That shine and glitter in the night.
The snow that's falling is getting deeper,
Hooray! I think that winter is here!

Rebecca Buchanan (8)
Maldon Primary School, Maldon

Winter Is Coming

Children wrapped up warm
In blue and sparkling pink,
The snow as soft as cotton,
Children having snowball fights.
But where's the snow?

Winter's breath, an icy air,
Following around the Earth.
It might come across a frozen lake.
But where's the snow?

The freezing blizzards from the Arctic zone,
Blast around you.
Thursday morning, February,
Wrap up warmly.
Here's the snow!

Beth Elsegood (9)
Maldon Primary School, Maldon

Winter

Wind slaps me like a spiteful child,
Car-shaped heaps of cotton wool,
Wind pushes me back
And pulls my coat like a bully.
But where's winter?

Icy branches like fingers,
Rain teardrops,
Snow is falling like pieces of cotton wool.
But where's winter?

Houses with icing sugar,
Wellington boots trudging in the snow,
Snow angels shaped like children.
There's winter!

Max Dee (9)
Maldon Primary School, Maldon

Winter?

Bobble-hatted children
Screams of delight
Scurrying down the hill
Having a snowball fight.
But where's the snow?
Cotton wool covers the ground
But none of the animals make a sound
The wind like an icy breath
But where's the snow?
A mountain of snow inviting a climb
A roof of thick icing
The bricks like an ice cube that never melts
Frozen lakes
But where's the snow?
Thursday morning, time to go
Wrap up warmly
Here's the snow!

Lucy Maynard (9)
Maldon Primary School, Maldon

But Where's The Snow?

The breath of icy caves
Children playing in snow
Flower-like hands
But where's the snow?

Blankets of snow
Frosty leaves
Someone is hiding
But where's the snow?

Elusive birds hiding away
Here comes the snow,
Hip hip hooray!

Jodie Butler (9)
Maldon Primary School, Maldon

It's Winter

The stone-like stream hard to touch,
The glacial water frozen for now,
The ice that was water.

(Oh! It's winter, it's winter.)
Not yet it isn't.

The insect-like children dancing in the snow,
The snow angels shaped like young ones,
The happy laughter of a child.

(Oh! It's winter, it's winter.)
Not yet it isn't.

The knife-like icicles hanging down,
The trees have their robes of snow on,
The holly bushes with their spikes.

(Oh! It's winter, it's winter.)
Yes it is, it is, it's winter.

James Dickson (9)
Maldon Primary School, Maldon

Where Is The Snow?

Prickly reaching branches
Stand with robes of snow,
Icing sugar stands freezing on top,
Dripping wet icicles hanging off the gripping hands.

But where's the snow?

Crystal clear lakes turning to ice,
The howling wind like a pack of wolves,
Birds echo everywhere, but nowhere to be seen.

But where's the snow?

Cave of frozen icicles,
Mounds of cotton wool,
Silent creatures, not a sound.

Here's the snow!

Corrin Jelbart (9)
Maldon Primary School, Maldon

Winter Will Be Coming

Bare frost trees touching the dark, gloomy, grey, crystal sky,
The frost whipping around in the midnight dark,
Winter will be coming.

Whipping wind rushing through faces,
A ghost going through,
A spit of cold on your shoulder,
Winter will be coming.

The crystal-blue in a sparkled eye,
A blue-white light,
Stone ice shizzing,
Winter will be here.

Snowflakes drifting down, lying a blanket
Winter here again.

Amy Harrison (9)
Maldon Primary School, Maldon

Where Are You Winter?

Children wishing to get ready to begin their snowball fights,
But no snow has fallen, not today nor last night.
Where are you winter?
Where are the snow angels that lay upon the landscape?
Where is the snow that settles on the windowpanes?
Where are you winter?
The trees poke up past the frost to reach the sunlight
Far above in the sky, past the clouds drifting by.
The snow has gathered into heaps like mighty mountains.
The children are all happy playing in the white, crispy snow.
Snowflakes are gliding down like dandelion seeds drifting beyond.
Here you are winter!
A white, frothy layer of pearly white snow.
The milky hills are covered with soggy footprints.
Animals hibernating, hiding from the icy wind.

Jasmine Linge (8)
Maldon Primary School, Maldon

Where Is Winter?

Icicles drop down to the frost underneath the bare trees.
The sound of invisible birds.
Bobble-hatted children having great fun.
Ice painted by Jack Frost.
But where's the snow?
Animals hibernating in any clean spaces.
Winter pulls the wind round and round.
Puddles turn into frosty ice.
But where's the snow?
Vehicles hiding, not to be found.
They are like bumpy mountains you could climb.
Ice-painted windscreens from Jack.
But where's the snow?
The whole week has passed.
No snow now.
It is Thursday, when I look out my window.
There is snow!

Joanna Crellin (9)
Maldon Primary School, Maldon

Winter

Puddles turn into frozen water
You can see yourself in the frozen ice
Ice-coated windscreens
But where's the snow?

The vehicles look like a blanket of snow
The vehicles spray the snow off the road
Car-shaped mounds of cotton wool
But where's the snow?

The houses look like they have been sprinkled with sugar
Just like a sugar cake
New footprints in the crisp snow
But where's the snow?

Ella-Mae Potter (8)
Maldon Primary School, Maldon

Where Are The Snowmen?

Children enjoying slippery puddles and jumping with joy.
Rain has gone, snow instead, skiing takes place on the blue,
But where are the snowmen?

The twittering birds, now fading,
Every moment the garden of green grows smaller
And patches of snow become bigger.
Last year just gravel, but this year snow.
But where are the snowmen?

Silvery ice scattered around,
The crunch of grass,
Snow lies on the kitchen floor.
Here are the snowmen!

Talasi Howell-Cole (8)
Maldon Primary School, Maldon

Where's Winter?

Children running in their woolly bobble hats.
Doing strong snow angels,
But where's the snow?
All the houses covered
In blankets of snow.
Windscreens frosty white.
But where's the snow?
Prickly tracks of cold,
Birds in the frost, clear snow.
But where's the snow?
The garden ponds are icy.
Here comes the snow.
Hooray!

Amy Curtis (8)
Maldon Primary School, Maldon

But Where's The Snow?

Children enjoying snowball fights,
Building snowmen,
Wrapped up warm like fire burning.
But where's the snow?

Snow as soft as cotton wool
And like flour spread around,
Icicles hanging from rooftops.
But where's the snow?

Grass tips turn white,
As you walk on grass it sounds like breaking crisps
And turns to the crisp of winter.
But where's the snow?

Frosted windscreens,
Cars are like snow monsters jumping out on you,
Just piles of snow.
But where's the snow?

Thursday morning, February,
Snow covers the ground, wrap up warmly.
Here's the snow!

Kiera Howell (8)
Maldon Primary School, Maldon

There's An Elephant Climbing Up My Tree

There's an elephant climbing up my tree
He is very nasty
He likes to eat nuts
And he says a lot of buts
It's an elephant.

There's an elephant climbing up my tree
His companion is a bumblebee
He tramples on the grass
And he likes to break glass
It's an elephant.

There's an elephant climbing up my tree
He eats like a chimpanzee
He goes to school every day
But sometimes he forgets his way
It's an elephant.

There's an elephant climbing up my tree
And it looks like he wants to eat me
He hates strawberry jam
But he quite likes ham
It's an elephant.

Ryan Whitehead (8)
Orchard Way Primary School, Croydon

My Dapple-Grey Horse

One day I saw my horse,
Looking straight at me,
On the way to the racing course,
1, 2, 3 . . .

Bang! went the gun,
My horse did a somersault,
I pulled back my horse,
Then he came to a halt!

I dismounted my dappled,
He reared up alone,
He then kicked out
And I broke a bone.

My leg went *snap!*
I collapsed on the floor,
I lay there motionless,
Like a sleeping boar.

Away they took me,
To see the doc,
No shoes on me,
Not even a sock.

My leg was so swollen,
It was bright red,
Mind, it could have been worse,
I could have been *dead!*

Eventually I came back to see,
My little dappled horse,
Then by limping very slowly,
I led him off the course!

Angela Petrassei (8)
Orchard Way Primary School, Croydon

My Dog

As I walk along the road
I really start to dream
I think of all the dogs
I like and think which one is best for me
Dalmatian, collie, Staffie or cross?
I really can't decide
I walk the streets and start to doodle
Then realise I'd love a *poodle*.

Abbie Thompson (9)
Orchard Way Primary School, Croydon

My Day At The Seaside

It's a hot day
At the seaside.
I'm so excited.
I built my sandcastle
And ate my ice cream.
I played with my shells
And watched the seagulls.
Swimming with the whales.

Rebecca Schneider (9)
Orchard Way Primary School, Croydon

Tiger, Tiger

Tiger, tiger orange and black
Tiger, tiger running in a pack
Tiger, tiger people running past
Tiger, tiger run very fast

Tiger, tiger *pounce!*

Becky Ward (8)
Orchard Way Primary School, Croydon

Space Is . . .

Space is about power on Neptune.
Space is flat on the moon
And it's very bumpy on the moon.
Space is silent.
Space is enormous and never ends.
Space is lonely and life-giving to stars.
Space is like a war on Mars, the red planet.
Space is dark and crowded on the Milky Way
With all the planets.
Space is an adventure on Jupiter, the gas giant.
Space is a place with space.

Jake Saunders (8)
Rockingham Primary School, Corby

Space Is . . .

Space is silent and dark
Because it has no living creatures,
Not one . . .
Not even humans,
Except aliens of course,
But they're not to be heard.
Space is a party,
Crazy, crazy party,
Because of comets whizzing around
And shooting stars,
Giving you good luck.

Elliott Chapman (8)
Rockingham Primary School, Corby

Space Is . . .

Space is rocky
Space is peaceful
Space is calm
Space is silent
Space is scary
Because it is dark
Space is lonely
Space is floaty
Space is dark
Space is enormous
Space is full of stars at night
Space has got lots of planets
Space is war
And the sun is very hot.

Chloe Morrison (8)
Rockingham Primary School, Corby

Space Is . . .

Space is dark like a park at night
Space is calm like a barn
Space is floaty like a coyote
Space is freaky and sneaky
Space is fab like a dad
Space is great like a cake.

Evan Williams (8)
Rockingham Primary School, Corby

Space Is . . .

Space is enormous but dark
Space is imaginary
Space is tremendous
Space is party planet
Space is cold and dark
Space is spooky and dark
Space is rocky but peaceful
Space is a place where
There are lots of shooting stars
Space is like Narnia but
Dark space is where you can't breathe
Space is a place where you can't remember
Space goes in slow motion
Space is flat
Space is lonely.

Jack Moir (8)
Rockingham Primary School, Corby

Space Is . . .

Space is starry
Space is sunny
Space is dark and scary
Space is happy
When it is lovely and calm
Space is rocky
Space is like a queen
And space is lovely.

Bethanie Forbes (7)
Rockingham Primary School, Corby

Taste

I love . . .
The taste of fizzy, fat lollipops tickling my tongue
The nibble of sweetly scented bubblegum,
stretching between my razor-sharp teeth.
The tangy taste of ripe, red strawberries
bulging with gooey chocolate sauce.
The meaty taste of super sizzling sausages
tumbling down in my stomach.

I love . . .
The fruity taste of tropical, luscious passion fruit
that has just come out of the electric blender.
The sugary taste of chocolate melting in my watering mouth.
I like the mellow fresh taste of a creamy milkshake
flowing freely down my throat.
I like the sour, tangy taste of curly, round oranges
peacefully rolling down my throat.

I love . . .
The spicy taste of peppery pizza being cut into slices
The sample of an icy cold drink on a boiling hot day
The refreshing, rancid taste of luscious, likeable lemons
being squeezed into juice.
But best of all is the hot, creamy taste of a caramel cake
drizzled with warm fudge sauce.

Jessica Hammond (10)
SS Peter & Paul RC School, London

Taste

I love . . .
The taste of vanilla ice cream,
Strawberry sauce is also nice.
Dreamy caramel makes me smile,
While chocolate fudge cake makes me go wild.
All I want is a lovely munch
Of this gigantic piece of fudge.

I love . . .
The flavour of the creamy dessert,
It has big waves of gold.
It looks like caramel ice cream,
But mostly solid gold.
I would eat it if it was ice cream
And dig out all the gold,
But it is not creamy ice cream,
So I'll just take the gold.

Kristian Medina (10)
SS Peter & Paul RC School, London

Sight

I love . . .
The sight of a clear blue sky lighting the world
The vision of a quiet sea on a calm summer's evening
The glow of the stars at night as I am stargazing through the galaxy
The shimmer of the sun, beaming down on the sunbathing bodies.

I love . . .
The glimpse of the white, cheesy moon spiralling in space
The view of a fresh, green meadow, the smell of the country
The display of large, solid buildings inhabiting the skies
But the appearance of my family is the best thing of all to see.

Kimberley-Anne Laylo (10)
SS Peter & Paul RC School, London

Smells

I love . . .
The smell of the blue sea, all sharp and salty
The perfume of new, fresh daisies growing in the garden
The odour of fresh snow tumbling into my hand
The fragrance in my kitchen when I'm baking luscious chocolate cake

I love . . .
The aroma of a freshly picked rose straight from the garden
The sniff of a lovely clean dog straight from a hot bath
The tang of a juicy, sharp lemon being squeezed into juice
But the scent of spicy sausages sizzling superbly in the hot pan,
Is the best of all.

Ashleigh Jones (9)
SS Peter & Paul RC School, London

Touch

I love . . .
The touch of golden sand slithering upon my hand
The feel of the leaves in autumn that are ripe on the tree
The understanding of the salty sea, that takes the lead
The style of designer clothes rubbing on the palm of my hand.

I love . . .
The texture of a Christmas tree tugged out of the earthy ground
Rubbing the skin of a scruffy dog
To embrace the hair of a black stallion galloping down the hill
To brush the hair of a puppy when it is in a deep sleep.

Juan David Tenorio (10)
SS Peter & Paul RC School, London

Taste

I love . . .
The taste of salty popping popcorn.
The juicy orange squirting juice into my mouth.
The delicious chewing gum, so very tangy.
The flavour of yummy chocolate cake watering in my mouth.

I love . . .
The cheesy pizza coming out of a hot oven.
The sweet smell of strawberries so delicious and yummy.
The tasty, salty chips which make me get big, fat lips.
The icy ice cream which makes me shiver.

I love . . .
The crinkly crisps so delicious and crunchy.
The fresh, red, ripe tomatoes squirting juice into my mouth.
The fresh-cooked bagels rolling out of the oven.
The crunchy biscuits crumbling in my mouth.

I love . . .
The sour, sizzling sausages jumping in the frying pan.
The tasty fairy cakes fluttering everywhere.
The scrumptious spaghetti spiralling everywhere.
The tasty eggs popping in the pan.

Lauren Wirrich (10)
SS Peter & Paul RC School, London

Taste

I love . . .
The taste of crispy pizza, fresh and hot out the oven.
The fresh, crispy chicken popping in my mouth.
The mouth-watering taste of a roast dinner on a lazy
                                      Sunday afternoon.
I love the elegant flavour of bubblegum squirting in my mouth.

I love . . .
The taste of fresh-baked brown bread sliding down my throat.
The delicious taste of strawberries tangling up my mouth.
The dignified taste of apple juice swirling in my mouth.
I love the taste of salty chips crinkling in my mouth.
I love the smooth taste of creamy butter on my bread.

Joe Scanlan (10)
SS Peter & Paul RC School, London

Smell

I love . . .
The smell of juicy oranges growing on the trees.
I adore the smell of sweet apple pie being baked in the oven.

I admire . . .
The smell of fresh, salty fish when it's being fried in the oven.

I love . . .
The smell of lollipops being scoffed on a summer's day.

I love . . .
The smell of perfume being sprayed all over the place.

Stephen Amat (10)
SS Peter & Paul RC School, London

Smells

I love . . .
The scent of sizzling sausages ready to be eaten.
The fragrance of grass that's just been cut.
The perfume of fresh flowers waving in the wind.
The incense of the blue, sharp, salty sea.

I love . . .
The aroma of new cars when I get in.
The whiff of fruit just been chopped up for people to eat.
The sweet smell of the Christmas pudding ready to be munched.
The redolence of a new, fresh day circling around me.

Ella Adkins (10)
SS Peter & Paul RC School, London

Smells I Love

I love . . .
The scent of shiny cherries hanging off a tree,
Running across a footpath just for me.
The perfume of fresh flowers growing and spinning in my garden.
The sweetness in the kitchen
When I bake a delicious chocolate cake.

I love . . .
The aroma of clean sheets when I'm cosy in the morning,
The smell of freshly squeezed orange splashing in my cup,
The whiff of oily chips whilst swimming in grease.

Connor Homer-Deegan (10)
SS Peter & Paul RC School, London

Taste

I like . . .
The taste of chocolate ice cream sliding down my throat.
The soft mashed potatoes bouncing up and down.
An appetising little nibble of meaty meat making its way to
                                            my empty stomach.

I like . . .
The delicious, salty fishfingers tumbling down to my belly.
The fresh, cold water swishing all the way.
The warm, sweet chicken popping everywhere.
But soft, cool ice poles are what I like the best!

Holly Dowling (10)
SS Peter & Paul RC School, London

Taste

I love . . .
The acid taste of tropical, dewy fruit,
The vinegary flavour of lollipops,
Juicy jam tarts being chopped down by my mouth,
Creamy cheesecakes jamming in my belly.

I love . . .
Hot, flaming, sickly pudding on my hand to my mouth,
Glacial North Pole ice lollies turning me to ice,
The sizzling pizza singing best friends forever
And the juice from a delicious watermelon.

Marley Christian Pompilio (10)
SS Peter & Paul RC School, London

Smell

I love . . .
The smell of crispy bacon frying in an oily pan
The perfume of silky lavender growing in the garden
The scent of fuming petrol being sprayed in a rusty old car
The sweetness of slimy shampoo being washed in fragranced hair

I love . . .
The smell of pouncing kittens having their fluffy fur groomed
The greedy hunting dogs chasing sly foxes
The whiff of crunchy brown bread wafting through the air coming
                                                            from the bakers
The incense of prawn cocktail crisps rattling in the packet.

Megan McDonald-Marshall (10)
SS Peter & Paul RC School, London

I Love . . .

I love the smell of fresh brown bread coming out of the oven,
The perfume of grass growing on my window sill,
The aroma of crackling pizza about to enter my mouth.

The sweet smell of chocolate right in front of my face, I approve,
Clean water in the sea with such a salty whiff,
Pepperoni pizza has a meaty, spicy smell, unlike other pizzas,
The attractive redolence of mouth-watering tomato soup lifts me
                                                          up into the air.

Oliver Togias (9)
SS Peter & Paul RC School, London

Smells

I love . . .
The smell of toasted bread being crunched.
The incense of fresh, normal shampoo on me.
The fragrance of cheesy pizza being eaten.
The stink of fiery cardboard being toasted to pieces.

I love . . .
The smell of cold, clean cars being washed.
The aroma of clean sheets snuggled up in bed.
The smell of sweet, yellow lemons being squeezed in people's faces.
The perfume of red, colourful roses being planted in the giant garden
Of the Queen.

Simone Mari (9)
SS Peter & Paul RC School, London

Tasty

I love . . .
The taste of magical, melting chocolate on a dark evening,
Of luscious, fresh, tropical pineapples, sweetened just for me.
I like sweet, juicy apples tingling down my throat,
Creamy caramel stirred deeply in chocolate.

I love . . .
The spice of stir-fry with meaty turkey for dinner,
The sour of jawbreakers popping in my mouth,
Of tangy sherbet fizzing through my body
And crunchy, brown bread baking in the oven.

Rosie Brooks (10)
SS Peter & Paul RC School, London

Taste

I love . . .
The cheesy relish of Hawaiian pizza,
Tumbling down into my mouth.
The savour of creamy caramel chocolates,
On a roller coaster through my tummy.
The mouth-watering morsel of scrumptious ice cream
Twirling through my throat
And the sip of soothing hot chocolate
Sliding through my body.

I love . . .
The piece of chocolate cake, spiralling around,
The sample of salty chips, fresh from the fryer,
The taste of cream soda, slipping down to darkness,
Also the crispy bacon, poured onto my plate.

I love . . .
Dreamy crackling eggs tumbling into space,
Oozing oranges exploding in my mouth,
Cheeky crisps flying like UFOs,
But to me, the delicious taste of Krispy Kreme doughnuts
Cannot be beat.

Pauline Villar (10)
SS Peter & Paul RC School, London

Taste

I like the taste of a strawberry smoothie,
Just the thing that makes me want to go to the movies.
The lovely flavour of a baked bread,
It all goes so lovely down my throat.

I adore the culture of a red tomato
Dancing and enjoying the freedom.
I sense the development of a fried chip,
It makes me go hyper when I eat it.

Claudia McCarthy (10)
SS Peter & Paul RC School, London

Five Senses

I love the flavour of juicy red strawberries
Covered in sweet brown sugar.
I adore the scent of hot chicken pie,
When it has just come from the oven,
The one that makes your bottom lip drop
And your mouth water uncontrollably.
I enjoy the peaceful sound of spring water
Pouring down a mountainside,
Clashing against the rocks
And then slowly and smoothly running along into the river.
I approve the feeling of an adorable hot shower
Tingling on my back,
Bouncing off onto the floor, following down the drain.

I care to see my friends at school
And to run around and jump and play with them
Until it is home time.

Elliott Fredrick (10)
SS Peter & Paul RC School, London

Taste

I love . . .
The taste of lovely pizza swirling in my mouth
The sweet, creamy chocolate ice cream gliding down my throat
The salty chips that my sharp teeth crunch down on

I love . . .
The scrumptious, juicy watermelon I eat filled with joy
The savoury golden bread baking in the boiling oven
The mouth-watering melon that turns around in my throat
The stylish chocolate cake sliding down my tongue.

Julia Mari (10)
SS Peter & Paul RC School, London

Taste

I love . . .
The taste of a cheesy pizza watering in my mouth
The fuzziness of a dark, fizzy Coke popping in my throat
The scrumptious caramel chocolate whirling in my mouth
And the fresh, soft ice cream jumping on my tongue

I love . . .
A piece of a creamy, chocolatey cake running down my mouth
The savour of a rich, crispy brownie crunching down my throat
The sample of a warm, salty chip somersaulting down my body
But the Krispy Kreme doughnuts are best of all.

Vanessa Zipagan (10)
SS Peter & Paul RC School, London

On The King Kang Kong
(Based on 'On the Ning Nang Nong' by Spike Milligan)

On the king kang kong
Where the cows go *nong*
And the monkeys all say *goo*
There's a kong kang king
Where the trees go *ling*
And the teapots libber labber loo.
On the kong king kang
All the mice go *clang*
And you just can't catch 'em when they do
So it's king kang kong
Cows go *nong*
Kong kang king
Trees go *ling*
Kong king kang
The mice go *shosh*
What a noisy place to belong
Is the king kang king kang kong!

Korede Falebita (7)
St Alban's Catholic Primary School, Hornchurch

On The Zang Zong Zing
(Based on 'On the Ning Nang Nong' by Spike Milligan)

On the zang zong zing
Where the ducks go *ming*
And the parrots all say *loo*
There's a zing zong zang
Where the hippos say *wang*
And the pigs say *bigger bagger boo*
On the zang zing zong
All the mice go wrong
And you just can't catch 'em when they do!
So it's zang zong zing
Ducks go *ming*
Zing zong zang
Hippos go *wang*
Zang zing zong
Mice go wrong
What a noisy place to be in
Is the zang zong zang zong zing!

Christopher Joseph Caballero (7)
St Alban's Catholic Primary School, Hornchurch

On The Ting Tang Tong
(Based on 'On the Ning Nang Nong' by Spike Milligan)

On the ting tang tong
Where the cows go *hong*
And the monkeys all say *too*
There's a gong gang ging
Where the trees go *ling*
And the teapots wibber wabber woo
On the tong ting tang
All the mice go *wlang*
And you just can't catch 'em when they do!
So it's ting tang tong
Cows go *hong*
Tong tang ting
Trees go *ling*
Tong ting tang
The mice go *wlang*
What a noisy place to belong
Is the ting tang ting tang tong!

Michael Webb (7)
St Alban's Catholic Primary School, Hornchurch

The Zoo

This morning when James walked into the yard
Chatter, chatter, chatter, chatter
About the zoo today.
As he approached the bus
Chatter, chatter, chatter, chatter
About the zoo today.
As we approached the zoo
Chatter, chatter, chatter, chatter
About the zoo today.
As we got off the bus, a herd of children
Hustled into the zoo today.

Matthew Collins (10)
St Cuthbert's RC Primary School, Walbottle

My Sister, Amy Claire Hodge

A mazing
M arvellous
Y oung

C lever
L oving
A ce
I ncredible
R adical
E xcellent

H ilarious
O verwhelming
D rama queen
G orgeous
E xciting.

Jessica Hodge (10)
St Cuthbert's RC Primary School, Walbottle

A World Inside A Box

Once upon a time there lived a world inside a box,
Where no rabbits were chased by a fox,
With the reddest flowers and bluest skies,
Where the fiercest cats played with butterflies.
A world filled with animals,
What could go wrong?
Nothing . . .
In a world filled with happiness for so long.
For thousands of years this world existed,
But for the first time ever, the lake misted.
Suddenly, there was a crack in the sky
And standing there was Mrs Fry.
Shocked, she peered inside the box
And thought she had found Heaven.

Jenny Brown (11)
St Cuthbert's RC Primary School, Walbottle

The Dragon

Soaring slowly above our heads,
The dragon flies while we sleep in our beds.
About the size of a double-decker bus,
We are nothing compared to it,
As it greedily eyes us up.
We sleep on unaware
That this young dragon pup
Has come to gobble us up.
As it silently flies over a house,
It licks its tongue across the wall,
Smelling the tender humans inside,
Ready to meet their fall.
A silent swoop,
A fiery cough,
A raging inferno bursts forth,
Incinerating everyone who sleeps
In the house on the hill.

James Hall (10)
St Cuthbert's RC Primary School, Walbottle

My Cat

I have a cat,
Who's rather fat,
Though he can climb up trees,
Where he bothers busy bees,
And when you get to know him,
You will want to get going,
Because he mauls your feet,
As he thinks you're tasty meat.

Georgia Stone (11)
St Cuthbert's RC Primary School, Walbottle

Pearl The Cat

In a room dark and silent, there is a cat,
The family cat.
Sleepily dozing after a good day's work,
Chasing and making people laugh.
Suddenly, she disappears,
I wonder where?
On a chair? Eating a plant?
Where did she go?
To the living room to take a nap,
With a golden-brown paw over her head,
She sleeps,
For she is the fourteen-year-old,
Family cat.

Francesca Giuliani (11)
St Cuthbert's RC Primary School, Walbottle

Happy Heart

I have a necklace that's been passed
Down my family for years,
And when I'm sad or lonely,
It fills me with cheers.

My necklace is silver,
It gleams in the sun,
The diamonds on it,
Shout out to everyone.

When I wear it,
My troubles melt away,
Locked up in a box,
So happiness won't go astray.

Chloe Kendal (11)
St Cuthbert's RC Primary School, Walbottle

Winter

Bleak,
Cold,
Icy,
Chilly,
Frozen,
Dull,
Snowy,
Wintry.
These are the words that best describe winter.
The snow, the sadness, the bleakness
And the icicles like splinters.
The fights on the streets
(With snowballs of course!)
This is winter,
The most melancholy season of all.

Chalon Collingwood (11)
St Cuthbert's RC Primary School, Walbottle

Grace

My cousin Grace is very cute,
She's only five years old.

Grace is very good indeed,
She does everything she's told.

Her hobby is Irish dancing,
She has magical dancing feet.

When the music starts,
She feels her heart,
Dancing to the beat.

Katherine McKeen (11)
St Cuthbert's RC Primary School, Walbottle

The Sky

The sky above us is so high,
Up there like a blueberry pie.

Or spread out like blue butter,
If it could talk, maybe it would stutter.

The home of cushiony clouds,
Or puffy pillows that make no sound.

It's also the home of a light source,
That probably won in a yellow assault course.

Is it orange? No! Is it red? No!
It looks like a comfy, blue bed.

Alexander Dundon (10)
St Cuthbert's RC Primary School, Walbottle

A Car

It can sound like a bulldozer,
It's loud, so loud.
It's fast, it tastes of metal
And it smells of petrol.

It feels as if it has lumps.
It's as fast as a motorbike.
It can be blue, yellow, red, silver
Or almost any colour.
It's shiny and so bright,
It can almost blind you.

Arran Yau (11)
St Cuthbert's RC Primary School, Walbottle

Picture Day

Every year in May,
My mum would turn and say,
'Tidy your hair,
Decide what to wear,
Today it's picture day.'

I'd fake a bad disease,
And say I'd cut my knees,
But she'd say, 'No!
You've got to go!
And get a good photo, please!'

My heart went rather wild,
And all my nerves compiled,
A guy with photography gear,
Positioned my year
And photographed each child.

When I saw the snap he'd taken,
I swore he was mistaken,
A photo of me?
This couldn't be!
I looked like a sack of bacon!

When my mum saw the school photograph,
She couldn't help but laugh!
She chuckled and giggled,
And chortled and wiggled,
And laughed till she broke in half!

Alannah Taylor (9)
St Joseph's RC Primary School, Waltham Cross

Spring Offspring

The first sun is too compressed,
Giving werewolves increased time to howl.
But soon the sun relaxes by stretching itself,
Giving owls less time to hoot.
The farmers' crops grow better
And the grains of rice are well watered
As green fills every tree.
Coloured flowers sprinkle on fresh green trees.
The time expands by an hour!
How mysterious!
The fruits are fresh and green
And honey is reunited with its owners.
Full of energy are birds and bees,
Delivering pollen from flower to flower,
As spring ebbs away, its effect gets better.

Mahfuzur Rahman (10)
Stamford Hill Primary School, London

Beach Poem

A big, bright, shining sun gleaming on my cheeks,
Children playing, children jumping,
Everybody walking up and down,
Aeroplanes appear in the blue, bright sky
And the days go past.
People crying, people laughing,
New season, a better place to be.
Children shouting, children whispering,
What a nice place to be!
But every day is a better place to be,
You can hear the whales go swish, swish, swish,
You can hear the birds talking
And if you come, you may hear them as well!

Ayanna Tafial-Novella (10)
Stamford Hill Primary School, London

Shoes

Shoes, shoes come in all shapes and sizes,
Sometimes you get them as surprises.
Short, tall, skinny, fat,
There is Nike, Fila, Reebok,
They've got so many names.
In a market they have a lot of shoes,
I don't know which ones to choose.
There's JD, Footlocker and a million more,
Walthamstow Wood Green galore
Shoes, shoes are everywhere.
But when you finally choose a pair,
They say they're not there!
Then you'll turn to your mum and dad
And say, 'It's not fair!'
And they'll say, 'There, there, dear.'
So like I said,
Shoes come in all shapes and sizes.

Altiman James Jnr (11)
Stamford Hill Primary School, London

Summer

Children playing on the beach,
Water slashing on the rocks,
Seagulls singing,
Happy families together laughing,
Birds sitting on roofs,
Kids playing together peacefully,
Families riding horses,
People resting,
Machines running,
Food going fast,
People going,
Sunset coming,
No sound to be heard.

Kenny Tran (11)
Stamford Hill Primary School, London

My Ideal World

Hot, exotic, the wind blows
The tropical island
The sweet tropical garden
The sea so bright, the fishes glow
The beautiful island made out of gold
The heavenly birds sing a sweet song
The dishes of fruit so sweet and warm
The peace and quiet so lovely and alone
The dark approaches
The sweet sound of the breeze
The nice food, so sweet out of the garden
The fruits so soft that the birds eat and sing
Have a dip in the pool, the air so soft
Sitting in the sun getting a tan
The fresh air blows along with the waves
The hot, exotic tropical island.
Ahkeisha Brown (11)
Stamford Hill Primary School, London

Summer

The sun appears every day when you are not expecting it.
Grass sparkles as the evening goes by.
Places are often getting sun, attracting from windows.
People love the sun and that makes them want to sunbathe.
Days have the effect of making people have a feeling for the
                              glistening grass and sun.
Sometimes, when you are cooking in the kitchen in the summer
And you have got the blinds up, the sun will shine in your face.
Little kids have a feature for the sun.
Meezan Paul (10)
Stamford Hill Primary School, London

Families

Love may be forever, but life is too short.
People go to Heaven and people go to Hell.
We may all have regrets,
But in the end life is too short for regrets.
We must always have faith
Because faith leads us to life and strength.
All we need to have in this world is love and peace.
Respect health and safety and each other.
We need to trust ourselves to trust others.
God is watching over us, just as we speak.
God can forgive us so we can forgive each other.
Selfish people, rude people, racist people,
All know what they have said and done.
And now is the time to put it all right.
We can choose our friends, but we can't choose our families,
But they are our flesh and blood.
We have to accept that it's too late to regret,
But now is the time to complete all our dreams,
Before it's too late.

Davika Gravillis (11)
Stamford Hill Primary School, London

It's Summer!

The sun gets lighter
The sky goes blue
My skin changes
Just like the weather.
Summer is brighter
Life goes sweeter
Days become longer
Time becomes slower.
When the weather is welcoming
You know it's summer.
If there wasn't a season called summer
Life wouldn't be the same.
When it's summer we get together
People dance and sing.
That's why I say summer is the best season.
Summer is a season of enjoyment
So let's play.

Kadiatu Kamara (11)
Stamford Hill Primary School, London

One To Ten

One orange octopus often occupied the old owl in October.
Two terrible tourists translate Turkish and had a tantrum on a train.
Three triangular tanks travelled through the town.
Four frightened, fresh frogs flipped and flopped to the floor for
food and fun.
Five fleeting flies flew furiously to Florida.
Six singing sparrows sat on speckled sticks.
Seven smelly, spotted spiders scared six silly servants.
Eight evil eagles eating eggs.
Nine naughty gnomes nicked new necklaces from nice nannies.
Ten tall tortoises terrified the trotting toddlers.

Gold Class (Year 4)
Thomas Fairchild Community School, London

My Pets

I've got a crocodile as my pet
She's the nicest animal I've ever met!
I've got an elephant as my pet
When I put him in the bath he gets me wet!
I've got a pet monkey
And he's very funky.
I've got a pet giraffe
And she makes me laugh.
They are my pets.

Elle Russell (8)
Thorpedene Junior School, Shoeburyness

I Thought These Things Were Not Real

There's pixies in the pantry
A dragon in my bed
I live in a castle on a cloud
The place is such a madhouse!

I didn't know about these things
But then again I thought those dinosaurs were dead
And when it's such a gloomy day
The clowns are never at a delay
My terrible day they turn around.

I always used to find it a dream
Until that day with an alien beam
It was big and it was scary
Especially that monkey, he was big and hairy.

There's zombies in the bathroom
And I think they're about to rise very soon
One day I think I might just scream
But then again, I could just get rid of the beasts
Well, I mean the leprechaun at least
And then I could just live a life of ease!

Tyler Crawley (11)
Thorpedene Junior School, Shoeburyness

World War Two

World War Two was horrible
Aeroplanes crashing, banging every night
Bombs going off night after night
German planes
People scared every night
Every night enemy planes.

Jenna Waterman (8)
Thorpedene Junior School, Shoeburyness

Back In Time

Way before I was born,
The Egyptians made pyramids and sphinx and bread,
And mummified bodies when they were dead.

Long, long ago,
The Viking slaves worked as hard as they could,
For their masters, collecting wood.

Before I was alive,
The Tudors had houses which were very posh,
But they didn't often wash!

Many years ago,
To school the children came,
If they were naughty, they would get the cane.

Before anyone I know was born,
In World War I there were bombs banging
And fires crackling.

My grandma and grandpa were in World War II,
Bombs were dropped from planes
And it wasn't fun and games.

When I was two,
I couldn't see the point of crawling
Because I might have been falling.

But now,
I'm having fun
And I love to run!

Laura Joseph (8)
Thorpedene Junior School, Shoeburyness